Soul Survivors:

From Trauma to Triumph

Edited by Lynn C. Johnston

A Whispering Angel Book

Soul Survivors: From Trauma to Triumph

Copyright © 2016 by Whispering Angel Books as an anthology.

Rights to the individual stories and poems reside with the authors themselves. This collection contains works submitted to the Publisher by individual authors who confirm that the work is their original creation. Based on the authors' confirmations and the Publisher's knowledge, these pieces were written as credited. Whispering Angel Books does not guarantee or assume any responsibility for verifying the authorship of any work.

Views expressed in each work are solely that of the contributor. The publisher does not endorse any political viewpoint or religious belief over another.

All rights reserved under International and Pan-American copyright conventions. No part of this book may be used or reproduced by any means, graphic, electronic, or mechanical including photocopying, recording, taping or by any storage retrieval system without written permission of the publisher except in the case of brief quotations embodied in critical reviews and articles.

ISBN-13: 978-0-9839494-0-4

Whispering Angel Books
7557 West Sand Lake Road #126
Orlando, FL 32819

http://www.whisperingangelbooks.com

Printed in the United States of America

Whispering Angel Books is dedicated to publishing uplifting and inspirational works for its readers while donating a portion of its book sales to charitable organizations promoting physical, emotional, and spiritual healing. If you'd like to learn more about our books or our fundraising programs for your charity, please visit our website: www.whisperingangelbooks.com

"And once the storm is over you won't remember how you made it through, how you managed to survive. You won't even be sure, in fact, whether the storm is really over. But one thing is certain. When you come out of the storm, you won't be the same person who walked in."

~ Haruki Murakami

TABLE OF CONTENTS

DEDICATION iii

ACKNOWLEDGMENTS v

INTRODUCTION
Lynn C. Johnston vii

HIS EYE IS ON THE SPARROW!
Erika Hoffman 1

RARE JEWEL
Rene Hargett 4

A PERSISTENT SPIRIT
Kathleen A. Ryan 5

IN YOUR ARMS
Lynn C. Johnston 9

PLEA OF THE ADULT
Sharon Fulham 10

EYES
Bridget McNamara-Fenesy 11

SPRING STREET
Beth SKMorris 14

BLESSINGS IN DISGUISE
Daawy 15

SOMETHING HOLY

Cherise Wyneken 18

PROTECT ME

Jean Varda 19

IN THE RADIATION THERAPY ROOM

Lucinda Grey 19

JENNIFER

Deborah Lamkin Smith 20

JUST IN TIME

Sharon Fulham 22

FIGHTING INERTIA

Susan Mahan 24

MIRACLE

Lynn C. Johnston 25

JAIL: FREE

Joy Case, M.Ed. 27

BUTTERFLY

Alina Zeng 28

TO THOMAS

Carolyn T. Johnson 29

REBOUND

Theresa M. Leslie 31

FOR BETTER, FOR WORSE

Lisa Braxton 33

AFTER THE HURRICANE

Mary Laufer 36

LOST BUT NOT ALONE

Ruth E. Smith 37

SOMETHING DID SURVIVE

Lynn C. Johnston 40

MY JOURNEY OUT OF DARKNESS INTO LIGHT

R. Todd La Flame 41

SCAR TISSUE

Carolyne Van Der Meer 44

SURVIVING AFTER A MOMENT SHATTERS YOUR WORLD

Beckie A. Miller 45

THE WORST THING

Carolyn T. Johnson 48

ONE MORE TIME

Sharon Fulham 49

A TOUCH OF RED

Constance Gilbert 50

HARD LESSON

Anjali Pursai 53

ROCK ME

Jean Varda 54

THE GATES WERE OPENED

Anne Hill, Ph.D 55

GLIMMER OF HOPE

Lynn C. Johnston 59

PILGRIMAGE

Judith Lyn Sutton 60

AWAKENING

Rosemary McKinley 62

HEARTHSTONE

Karissa Dong 65

NOTHING LAST FOREVER, BUT

Wendy Wolf 66

THE OTHER SIDE OF THE STARS

Lola Di Giulio De Maci 68

FINDING MY RELIGION

Sheree K. Nielsen 70

ALONG FOR THE RIDE

Ann Reisfeld Boutte 73

WALKING

Theresa M. Leslie 76

HEALING FROM TRAUMA

Judy Shepps Battle 77

THE NURSE

Helen Carson 79

SPEAKING THE LANGUAGE OF MOMENTS

Roshanda Johnson 81

RELEASE

Aarya Mecwan 84

CHILD IN THE PICTURE

Lynn C. Johnston 85

KEEPSAKES

Jane Blanchard 86

SEEKING THE SPHERES

Rebecca Taksel 87

CARPE DIEM

Alina Zeng 90

I KNOW THAT I KNOW

Constance Gilbert 91

RELIEF

Aashna Belenje 94

A STRONG REBIRTH

Daawy 95

SMILING FROM ABOVE

    Lynn C. Johnston 97

JOURNEY

    Judith Lyn Sutton 98

THE WRITING THAT SHAPED MY LIFE

    Diana Raab Ph.D 100

MAYA ANGELOU, AN ANGEL OF HEALING

    F. Anthony D'Alessandro 103

A LIFE IN 5 MINUTES

    Juley Harvey 106

I WANT YOU TO LEAVE

    Cona Faye Gregory-Adams 110

THE NIGHT BREEZE

    Lynn C. Johnston 115

FRESHMAN TRYOUT

    Carol J. Rhodes 116

TWO WOMEN

    Judy Shepps Battle 119

BRIAN'S TREE

    Beckie A. Miller 122

THE EAGLE HAS LANDED

    Edward Louis 125

HOMECOMING
Anjali Pursai 127

SONNET 84 WE DO SUCCEED
E Baker 128

LISTEN UP
Ann Gilbreth 129

MEASURING UP
Susan Mahan 130

SURVIVE
Jim Pahz 131

HIS FAMILY'S CURSE
Skip Hughes 136

GRAVEN IMAGES
John Manesis 140

FLASHBACK
Michelle Shen 142

SACRED SUNSHINE
Rebekah Bernard 143

ABOUT THE CONTRIBUTORS 146

WE WANT TO HEAR FROM YOU 159

DEDICATION

"Never be ashamed of a scar. It shows you were stronger than whatever tried to hurt you."

~Unknown

This book is dedicated to the broken but resilient survivors among us who bravely tell their stories and reveal their scars proving the strength in our humanity lies in sharing our vulnerabilities.

ACKNOWLEDGMENTS

The creation and development of this book would not have been possible without the assistance of many people. I would like to thank everyone who submitted their heartfelt stories and poems for this anthology. With hundreds of wonderful pieces to choose from, each prospective contributor made the selection process far more challenging and rewarding than imaginable.

My deepest appreciation goes out to Leah Bergstrom, Ruth Marx, Tamara Seyhun, Patti Brown-DiPaolo, Del Berry, and Samuel Johnston. Your opinions and support have been invaluable during this process.

INTRODUCTION

The Greek philosopher, Plato, once said, "Be kind, for everyone you meet is fighting a hard battle." Those words never rang more true to me than when I was compiling this anthology.

All of our Whispering Angel Books anthologies focus on positive and inspirational experiences and life lessons we all can embrace; but when the inspiration for Soul Survivors spoke to my heart, I knew from the outset that this one would be a little different. I was asking our contributors to open up their hearts, show the scars that they probably spent most of their life denying their very existence, and then revealing how they used that pain to heal themselves and others. I was so honored and humbled that they trusted their personal experiences with me to share with the world.

The concept of Soul Survivors: From Tragedy to Triumph came to me last year while enduring my own series of traumatic events. In fact, it was this series of events that gave birth to the concept of Whispering Angel Books as I attempted to heal my own suffering.

On March 10, 2006, my world came to a screeching halt. I got a phone call from my parents that my mother, who was never sick a day in her life, a woman who was active and healthy, was suddenly diagnosed with pancreatic cancer. I remember standing in the kitchen with the phone pressed to my ear, knowing the survival rate is dismal. It was a heart-wrenching realization that my life would never be the same. Seven month later, she was gone.

Six weeks after the funeral, I was told that I was being laid off from my job. I was able to find a temporary position with promises that it would soon become permanent. But after a year, I was told that that job was also coming to the end too. It was now 2008 and massive layoffs were in the works throughout the country. It seemed everyone I knew was either unemployed or in fear of losing their job. As a single mother, I panicked not knowing how I was going to survive. After months of unsuccessfully looking for work, I launched Whispering Angel Books. I felt God spoke to my heart. If nobody else would hire me, I had to try to do it myself. I also needed to put something good, positive, and inspirational back into the world, not just for me, but for everyone else who knew was suffering. I wanted to create something that would give wonderfully gifted inspirational writers and poets an outlet to publish their works, touch the hearts of the discouraged and downtrodden while I could generate income for myself and allow me to contribute to charities that were uplifting our society. It was then the concept of Hope Whispers, the anthology on the power of hope and faith on physical, emotional, and spiritual healing, was born. Soon after came Living Lessons, Nurturing Paws, Littlest Blessings, and Miracles & Extraordinary Blessings.

Over the next three years, I desperately sought other work but found almost nothing. I landed temporary work for only six of those 36 months. As debts rose, my spirit plummeted and my troubles continued to ensue. My beautiful cat, Valentine, who you'll read about in the story, Miracle, who disappeared and was gone for three weeks. It was such a blessing to have her return to us. As of now, she is a happy, healthy 12-year-old cat.

But my troubles didn't end there. The financial strain of my lack of employment caused me to have to declare bankruptcy. It was a devastating realization as I had never missed a payment for anything in my life. My credit was pristine for 23 years and now it would be ruined.

I was also devastated by the fact that I no longer had the means to live life on my terms in California. My father, who was living in Orlando, Florida, at the time, said that if I moved there he could help support me until I could get back on my feet. Begrudgingly I had to accept his offer, but it broke my heart to know the life that I had built for myself had come to an end. The move itself was horrendous and to make matters worse another cat, Cross, disappeared two hours before my son and I were to get on the plane with them to fly to Florida.

I cried all the way to the airport heartbroken that I could not find Cross. I spent the next few days coordinating a search and rescue with my neighbors who understood my pain.

Fortunately, after nine days, like Valentine, he was found – another miracle. I was able to fly back to California to retrieve him.

I thought the worse was behind me and I could start rebuilding my life in a new state, but I was wrong. Three weeks to the day after arriving in Florida, my father died on a heart attack brought on by an adverse reaction to prescription pain medication he was given after skin cancer surgery.

That was five years ago, some things have been better and some things have gotten worse. Last summer as I felt the world crashing down around me, I plummeted into a deep depression. I truly didn't see a way out. I wouldn't say I was suicidal, but I had really started to feel that things would not improve. I cried out to God asking me to please help me, but I felt my pleas had fallen on deaf ears.

Then one night, after crying myself to sleep, I had a dream -- or as I believe -- a visitation. In this experience, I did not see anything but was swaddled tightly in the fetal position. It was like a big hug that got tighter and tighter as it went on. I had an overwhelming feeling of being safe, warm, and protected. I felt it from the crown of my head to the tip of my toes. As I basked in this embrace, I felt a surge of love infusing my spirit. It was like nothing I had ever felt before. In my heart, I felt my pain ease and I knew my pleas had indeed been heard on the other side. The embrace was so tight that I woke up convinced I would find myself tangled tightly in my bedding, but I was not.

The next day, I knew things would be different. My problems weren't solved, but now I felt like I had been heard. I could trust that God would see me through. I also knew that the love I felt infused with so deeply needed to be shared with others.

Soul Survivors: From Trauma to Triumph is dedicated to all the survivors. May you not suffer in vain, may you find triumph in your suffering, and may your victory be a beacon to all those still lost in the storm.

~ Lynn C. Johnston

"There is a sacredness in tears. They are not the mark of weakness, but of power. They speak more eloquently than ten thousand tongues. They are the messengers of overwhelming grief, of deep contrition, and of unspeakable love."

~ Washington Irving

HIS EYE IS ON THE SPARROW!
By Erika Hoffman

I didn't plan on surviving. The rip tide took me out further. I couldn't reach my husband. The salt water scorched my throat. The briny breeze kicked up the waves. The shore was a blur. No one was left on the beach at six pm, and I could barely spot the canopy in the distance where a wedding party had assembled a couple of hours earlier. No beachcomber strolled the shoreline, let alone swim in the ocean. Everyone had gone off to dinner. Though late in the day I didn't think it a bad time to have a quick dip.

That June afternoon, we weren't far out at all when a wave swept in and carried us to deep water. He's nine inches taller than I, but he couldn't touch bottom either, nor could he make headway against the surf. The water acting like a vortex pulled us down. Though not a great swimmer, I'd never feared drowning because I always knew I could breast stroke for a good 15 minutes. Up until that day, my swimming skills had sufficed. But this time I made no progress against the undertow. Nor could he. We were about thirty feet off shore when I knew I couldn't continue. Enervated from the 30-minute struggle, I told my husband I couldn't stay afloat. He began screaming for someone. Nobody heard him. He waved his arms, crossing them as he frantically sought help. No one saw us. I noted the panic in his eyes, and it reminded me of the desperate mien of a doe as a car barrels down on it. I knew it was over. I remember how sad I felt then that this was how it would end for me and most likely for him too. I recall imagining headlines in the local paper noting our deaths: *Caught in a Rip Tide*. I wondered if they'd say whether our bodies had been discovered. That became my wish: That our kids wouldn't think of us ripped apart by sharks and nibbled on by crabs. I prayed they wouldn't view our ravaged bodies. I wondered if they knew where deeds and important papers were stored so they wouldn't have trouble settling up an estate. Then, I sent up a prayer that they would live happy lives and not mourn us long or ruminate over the way they lost their parents. Our kids were still in their twenties, that age of independence, but they weren't yet settled with families and spouses of their own to comfort them through crises.

The water hit my eyes again and through my marred vision, I spied my husband a bit ahead of me. "Hold onto me!" I yelled as I felt myself being grabbed by the sea. He turned and reached back. With the tips of his fingers, he grabbed hold of the skirt on my bathing suit. "Don't let go!" I whispered, probably inaudible to him as the crash of the surf drowned out our words. Only the howling wind and the pounding of the swells on the beach could I hear. My head bobbed like a rag doll. I understood now what it meant when swimmers gave up because of exhaustion. My husband pummeled forward a bit, and then the wave's retreat took us back but we seemed not to fly back as far. The skirt on my suit stretched taut as the ocean greedily played tug of war with my husband. He moved further forward.

"My toe touched," he said. At that moment, I felt a glimmer of hope, faint and ephemeral. My husband pushed on, and I floated nearer to him. And we proceeded like that until he had my hand, and we waited for each wave to move us in a little and then he tried to hold the ground gained. Finally, he yanked me, and we collapsed at the edge of the sea. When he let go of my fingers, I feared I'd wash back into the greedy ocean. So with all my might I scratched my way up the hollowed out embankment. Most of my body then flopped lifeless on sand. The ebb and flow of the ocean wouldn't snatch me back. He stayed inert. My head burst. It throbbed like nothing I've ever felt before. It felt like a firecracker had exploded on the right side of my skull. I turned toward him and saw his face buried in the sand. I felt grainy morsels in my nose and felt my bathing suit edged up high on my legs, but I remained too weak to adjust anything. We lay. I figured we'd succumb soon. I was thankful our bodies could be found.

I don't know how long my husband and I slept. I seemed to go in and out of dreams. I recall gratitude: Now our kids would have bodies to bury, and they wouldn't wake in the middle of the night to terrors wondering where their folks' parts washed up. I heard a distant dune buggy and raised my chin slightly to see a life guard fly by up on top of the beach close to the dunes and houses, not near us. Could folks even spot us here lying below the cliff of sand, like half submerged detritus?

At some point, I asked my husband if he could get up. "Let me lie. My heart is racing," he murmured. Then, we fell back asleep.

Later that evening when the sun sank, we climbed up the slope and retrieved our flip flops and towels we'd left on the beach a long time back. As we mounted the steps leading to a boardwalk to the road, we ran into a couple with cocktails in hand who asked us if we were all right. I told them we nearly drowned, but my husband saved me. The man said a surfer had drowned that very day and another man the week before. Rip tides were frequent on this beach, he told us.

In the ensuing days, my headache didn't get better, and my sense of balance worsened. I started having trouble typing stories. I seemed stuck in a perpetual fog. We went to the hospital for me to have a CAT done. It showed that a pool of blood had collected on one of my brain's lobes, caused by burst capillaries. The capillaries broke because of a surge of adrenalin that erupted when I clawed my way up the bank. An MRI was scheduled for two days after the CAT. Before that second test happened, I had a seizure in which I dropped to the floor. My left side went numb, and my left hand curled unnaturally over my chest. En route to the hospital, I accepted my fate---that I would be paralyzed forever. As I mused on this "life after life," I was all right with the idea of being confined to a wheelchair. I surmised I could become a Wal-Mart greeter in this next stage of my mortal journey. I pictured myself at the entrance to a mammoth store waving at folks with my right hand, and in my mind's eye, I was smiling as I said hello to shoppers.

It sounds funny now to repeat the reveries I had as my husband whisked me down the road to the ER. I felt gratitude that I was alive.

My paralysis was temporary. The blood absorbed within months, and I was back to my old sassy self.

What I learned en route to the emergency room was that I would survive whatever setback I encountered. I had survived drowning, and I'd survive this stroke. Life was good, and I'd be happy. I decided I'd make the best of any situation that comes my way.

Now when some unforeseen event happens that might seem like a major upheaval to another woman, I think how lucky I am – lucky to be alive. It might sound corny or sappy, but once you survive something that could have ended your human life, you find an inner strength and a knowledge that you will go on.

Gloria Gaynor's song, "I Will Survive" resounded with a lot of folks not only because of its peppy tune and great message but also because it touched some at a deeper level. A person feels she might survive again if having lived through a major crisis or setback once before. A woman knows that another disaster could come her way but she's now more prepared for the next challenge life tosses. "Bring it on!" could be the sequel to "I Will Survive!" Or maybe, better yet as follow-up to "I Will Survive" would be a catchier remake of the hymn, "His Eye in on the Sparrow."

 My near miss let me know He's watching me. And I am grateful.

RARE JEWEL
By Rene Hargett

From the outside in shame covered me
I felt I was no longer what I use to be
My frame had altered greatly and with it came despair
Fear and judgment consumed me and then controlled my air.
No longer could I go outside to even meet with GOD
Self-loathing stole my peace and sleep and replaced it with a need to hide
But there in the midst of the dark and the pain I heard GOD'S voice speak clearly
"Have you forgotten daughter what matters most to ME?
The love you have within your heart is what I'M looking at
The way you smile and care for others and when I bless you, the way you bless back
The way you shine as the jewel I created though I work to perfect you continuously
Seeking to obey every word I have stated, the precious way you've chosen to love on ME
Understand my daughter and look at what I see
The rarest of my jewels is what I'VE created you to be
And every jewel that I create
Has a different size and a different shape...
Every package for MY jewels I have chosen too
And when that package alters I don't hold it against you
Just follow MY instructions for the package you are in
And know the best part of the package is the rare jewel that's within."

A PERSISTENT SPIRIT
By Kathleen A. Ryan

The signs began within a couple of hours of my brother's death.

These signs, which could be construed as coincidences, have been extremely comforting since the devastating loss of my 37-year-old brother on May 20, 2001, when he was killed in a motorcycle crash, just days before his fifth wedding anniversary. On this contradictory bright and warm Sunday, with the fresh smell of spring in the air, he left behind a 30-year-old widow, their five-month-old son, and an immeasurable number of family and friends who continue to grieve his loss.

The theories surrounding coincidences and synchronicity date back thousands of years. Scientists, philosophers, and mathematicians have pondered their existence. Even Hippocrates believed the universe was joined by "hidden affinities." For centuries, meaningful coincidences were seen as omens or messages from the gods. Among others, the topic has been explored by Wolfgang Pauli, Carl Gustav Jung, Paul Kammerer, and Deepak Chopra.

I've experienced it firsthand.

While identifying my brother's body in the hospital, a feeling overwhelmed me; that before me appeared the shell of who once was my brother. He wasn't trapped inside his dead body; it wasn't him any longer. His soul had already departed. With these realizations, an unexpected calmness came over me. Crying, I kissed his cheek, caressed his face, and said goodbye to my beloved baby brother, telling him how much I loved him.

When the coincidences began, it convinced me that a consciousness exists beyond the grave. The synchronistic events are welcomed and reassuring, but none more so when three years later, I faced a breast cancer diagnosis and endured a long road of surgeries, chemotherapy, and radiation treatments.

Apparently, coincidences can occur in clusters. As part of my pre-surgical testing, I had an EKG. When the young female technician finished the test and I began getting dressed, she asked, "Are you returning to work after your mastectomy?"

"Yes — I'm a police officer, and I plan to return to work as soon as I'm healed. I answer a tips line and take anonymous calls from the public to help solve crimes and locate wanted persons."

She listed the names of several officers she knew, whose names were unfamiliar to me. I explained, "I work in headquarters; if these officers work in patrol, our paths don't usually cross."

She offered to walk with me to my chest x-ray. She resumed our earlier conversation. "Oh – my cousin works in the Sixth Precinct," she said, without mentioning his name. She probably assumed I wouldn't know him, either.

I felt compelled to ask. "What's his name?"

"Alex Sanchez."

I stopped in my tracks. Had I still been attached to the EKG, she would have detected my heart skipping a beat. My hand covered my mouth as I shook in joyous disbelief. She paused and turned towards me, with a quizzical look on her face. Trying to get the words out, I couldn't help but stutter. "He is the officer who handled my brother's fatal motor vehicle accident! You don't understand what this means to me — on top of what happened yesterday at work. I learned that a tip I took resulted in a murder arrest. The arrest report indicated that the victim was murdered on May 20, 2001, the same day my brother was killed. They entered heaven on the *same* day!"

My brother was working overtime trying to get through to me. My fears about the pending journey began to dissipate; I immediately felt that everything would be all right.

Little did I know he was just warming up.

A week after my mastectomy, the breast surgeon said the margins were clean, the lymph nodes tested negative, and a lump removed from the right breast was benign. Relieved at such good news, I assumed it meant a lighter form of chemotherapy, and a chance to keep my hair.

No such luck.

My medical oncologist said I'd receive the most severe form of chemo available, trying to blast any budding cancer cells out of my body for good. As a wife and mother of two, I was thrilled to be alive, but still dreaded the eventual hair loss and illness.

"However," he advised, "you're not healed enough from surgery to start chemo yet, so you must schedule another appointment."

He gave the same response during the second visit.

After receiving two reprieves, I feared the third appointment, knowing the oncologist would set a starting date — with baldness and nausea to follow. I remained alone in the waiting room for about forty-five minutes, then I was led to an examining room where an additional forty-five excruciating minutes ticked by. The pressure mounted, and repetitive thoughts of inevitable hair loss and the misery of chemo agonized me. I broke down and cried.

A nurse walked into the room. She asked, "Uh-oh – what's the matter?"

"I'm going to start chemo soon, and it's beginning to hit me."

She advised, "After your appointment, stop in to see the social worker. Her office is down the hall, the last one on the right."

I wasn't going to bother, but after receiving the dreaded news, with an ironic starting date of April Fools' Day, I walked down the hall to pay the social worker a visit. Her door was open, and she was seated behind her desk. She rose to meet me and extended her hand. As we shook hands, I recognized her immediately.

"You're Darlene Ernest, aren't you?" I asked.

"Ernest is my maiden name; I recently married. Have we met before?"

"Three years ago — on May 20, 2001, in the emergency room of this hospital. My brother was killed in a motorcycle accident, and you had given my mother grief counseling information. In fact, you were the first sign from my brother the day he died. My uncle had noticed your name tag and mentioned it after you left the room. My brother's name was Ernest. After meeting you again today, I believe it's another sign from my brother."

Visibly moved, Darlene said, "I believe today *is* another sign; I have to tell you something." Her eyes widened as she spoke. "I worked just *one week* in the ER that year to cover a social worker's vacation. I normally work *here* – I'm assigned to oncology."

As the chemo treatments neared, my anxiety level rose. I had a dream one night that I will never forget.

In the dream, I was driving a car, headed for my first chemo treatment. I was waiting to make a left turn out of a gas station, but the traffic kept coming. Suddenly, a car stopped; the driver angled his car in the street in such a way to prevent motorists from passing. He even got out of his car and stood in the roadway. I exited the station, and turned my head around to wave and thank the driver. *It was my brother.* My first thought was to pull over and run to him, but I saw him get back into the car. He turned his vehicle around to drive behind me. I adjusted my rear view mirror to watch him. He was behind me all the way to the hospital for my first chemo treatment.

He was behind me all the way.

I worked throughout my chemotherapy and radiation treatments. I wore wigs and colorful bandanas to complement my outfits. I discovered that losing my hair and occasionally feeling nauseous was a small price to pay in exchange for a chance to extend my life. I took it all in stride. After all, how could I complain when this was the path I needed to take in order to survive? I was battling cancer, fighting for my life – I couldn't worry about what people thought if they saw me wearing a wig or a bandana.

Besides, I had a persistent spirit in my corner. As coincidences and signs from my brother continue, it fills me with awe. I welcome the whispers of his soul with a smile and I am comforted, knowing he is near and remains a part of my life.

IN YOUR ARMS
By Lynn C. Johnston

As a child I used to dream
Of a magical place where no one would scream
Where the sunshine warmed my freckled face
And memories of pain could all be erased

Where the soft breeze would blow through my hair
And I could walk without a care
Where the sand would seep between my toes
And I could hide from my painful woes

As the water lapped against my feet
My heart could recover from hurt and defeat
Swaddled in a blanket, the world shut out tight
No matter the pain I would be all right

A place that only existed in my young mind
That as I grew up became harder to find
The older I got I couldn't pretend
And wounds left by life needed much more to mend

That world disappeared as age took its place
Until the day it returned in your sweet embrace
In your arms I feel safer than I ever did then
And I can thank God I need no longer pretend

PLEA OF THE ADULT
By Sharon Fulham

Like a tired thirsty turtle, I ease out of my shell
Please treat me fairly, and please treat me well

I come open-hearted, down a path old and new
With high expectations my dreams will come true

I have years of experiences engraved on my back
Winds brutal have battered, but still I'm intact

My faith has been tested, if my soul you could see
The worst is behind me; the best yet to be

Tread ever so softly on things that I share
Don't judge me too harshly if you haven't been there

Do regard my perspective, I have insurance you see
I've learned from the struggles life has hammered on me

I am here to gain knowledge. I am not here on trial
This could be my last chance to do something worthwhile

I implore you to listen, hear what I don't say
As I gather new milestones along this pathway

If you'll respect my footsteps and accept who I am
I will give you my best and do all that I can

I want to inspire others who have something to tell
And give them a reason to ease out of their shell

EYES
By Bridget McNamara-Fenesy

We stepped into the harsh sunshine, and I held back tears as Paige buried her face in my shoulder.

"It hurts, Mommy."

"I know baby. Daddy and I are trying to find out why so we can fix it."

I settled Paige into her booster seat, gently placed her blanket over her head to block the light, and said quietly to Jeff through clenched teeth, "How could a man who claims to be a doctor suggest that our daughter's problem is that she sleeps with *one* eye open? That's insane!"

"Yes, it is," agreed Jeff. "I'll be right back." He left us as he crossed the street to a convenience store. He emerged a minute later with a magazine in hand, flipping through the pages.

As he opened the car door, he handed the open magazine to me. "There – under 'Specialists: Pediatric Ophthalmology' – call that one." I flipped to the cover of the magazine – it proclaimed its annual list of Portland's best doctors.

I told the voice that answered my call about my four-year-old's sudden onset of severe sensitivity to light. How one of her eyes was so red it appeared mauled. How we kept our house as dark as possible, but she ate her meals in her bedroom closet where no light could get in. How we'd been to four doctors and nobody could help and it was getting worse by the day.

After waiting on hold for what felt like an eternity, the receptionist picks back up. "The doctor says to come in – she'll see her right now."

We crossed town and entered the doctor's office. The woman at the front desk showed us immediately to an exam room, took our basic information, and within moments the doctor entered.

She didn't make small talk, but went immediately to Paige. Paige tried to keep her eyes open while the doctor peered in, cooing reassurances. I could tell that the pinpoint light the doctor was shining in her eyes was excruciating. Paige turned to me, silently pleading. I looked back at her, helpless, offering only love, which didn't seem enough.

The doctor scooped Paige into her arms and told her she was going to let her play with some toys while she talked with Mom and Dad.

"I'd like Paige to see a cornea specialist," she said when she returned, closing the door behind her.

"A scratched cornea? That sounds pretty fixable," I said, relieved. "Do you have someone we can call for an appointment?"

"No – we don't have that luxury. I've already called him. He wants to see her now. In fact, he's on his way."

"He's on his way here? What? Is he a part of your practice?"
She shook her head no.
"Why would he come here?"
"Because if this is what I think it is, there is no time to lose."

A crushing pause. Jeff slipped his hand over my own, icy cold, white at the knuckles.

"I believe Paige has corneal herpes. It's rare – this is the first case I've seen in a child. But it is serious - in a word, the herpes virus is eating her cornea. If we don't arrest it, Paige will be blind in a matter of days."

The room reeled.

The specialist, Dr. Ferrin, saw Paige and again dismissed her to the play room.

He turned back toward us, confirmed the diagnosis, and advised that while the virus was currently only active in one eye, there was evidence it had migrated to the other. He gave us multiple prescriptions with instructions to get them filled on the way home. "Paige needs a dose of this one right away, and this one must be given every four hours – including through the night."

"Wake her up? She hates taking medicine." The import of what he was saying refused to sink in.

"If you think that you won't be able to get these medicines in her, we'll admit her to the hospital tonight."

"No. We can do this." There was an immovable stone in my throat.

Dr. Ferrin handed us his card. "Here's my office. I will see you tomorrow morning at eight." He squeezed my shoulder: "I don't think it's too late – at least for one of her eyes. I promise you we will do everything we can to save her sight."

I tried not to cry as I went to gather Paige and place her oh so gently back in her car seat.

For several weeks, we began every morning – including weekends and when Doc was supposed to have gone on vacation, in his office – always at eight, before the office was open so he could spend time with Paige. The steroids relieved the inflammation and light sensitivity within a matter of days, but he wouldn't offer us a victory on any other front. He monitored Paige's eyes with the vigilance of an army captain in the midst of battle. He spoke with us about the possibility of a corneal transplant.

I went home and looked it up on the Internet. Success rates were terribly low.

"Probably even lower in children," he confirmed the next morning. "But it may be all we've got. This virus is not giving up. But I'm not either." He upped the dosages of her meds despite her tiny size.

I took a leave of absence from work. My job became saving Paige's eyes. I found myself pointing out colors, patterns, everything to her. We read books, and I spelled out words, lingered over pictures. I pushed off the dark fear that lived with me, that maybe she wouldn't be able to see any of this soon – that I needed to imprint her memory. I monitored her medicine with a vengeance. I rearranged my schedule so that each medicine was delivered at exactly the right time. I bargained that if kept to the schedule, I'd be rewarded with her sight. I cried regularly, but never in front of her. Doc said we needed to keep her stress level low – stress triggers the virus. All Paige knew was that she had to go to the doctor to be "checked" every day.

After many more weeks, when the repetitiveness of the daily routine had left us walking through each day in a semi-conscious stupor – Doc lifted his head from his microscope, pushed over to peer in Paige's no longer sensitive eyes, and turned to us.

"I can't tell you how close this was. But I think we got it. Paige is going to be okay."

For the first time since our ordeal began, Paige watched as I wept.

My daughter is now thirteen years old. If you look very closely, you see the tiny cloud on her right eye near her pupil – the nearly invisible reminder of her battle. Every morning at breakfast, and every night before bed, she takes her little blue anti-viral pills to keep the monster that lurks in her cells at bay. She knows that at the slightest sign of redness – even if it's likely only a cold – we have to go directly to the doctor. She will take her meds for the rest of her life.

But now, every morning when I wake her, and she looks back at me with a smile, I am grateful that we didn't believe that a child could sleep with one eye open, that there are doctors that will drop everything to help, that she will be able to see her own child one day and tell about her close call. With eyes wide open.

SPRING STREET
By Beth SKMorris

first visit to the Warehouse site
since 2002. I sit down at the bar in an Irish pub
that's been on Spring Street since 1817, order
a salad and a shot of whiskey. Lunch-time
crowds filled with Wall Streeters; making deals,
comparing workouts, chatting up the sun-bronzed legs,
six-inch espadrilles at the next table. Ten minutes ago
I was standing in the center of the 'Dedication Room'
at the Fire Museum up the street,

immersed in pictures
and stories of the 343 fire fighters who
lost their lives on 9/11. No monumental
museum, this is a memorial to their own-
personal, intimate. The docent encouraged
me to watch the video in the next room.
We sat for a while sharing tears, history.
She handed me a box of tissues, told me-
Take all the time you need.

Noisy laughter, loud voices
pull me back. I wonder if the young people
behind me give any thought to what happened
down this street, west of this corner fourteen
years ago? Maybe they do. Maybe they lost
someone dear to them. Maybe Uncle Jim
from Engine Company No. 42, but today
the talk is all about sales prospects, tennis
elbows, summer hot-spots.

I turn and smile at them, belt down what's
left of my whiskey, pay my bill, walk east,
passed the Warehouse towards the subway.

BLESSINGS IN DISGUISE
By Daawy

The man with the gun was in my bedroom. He came to find me. In the name of mercy, I screamed at him to pull the trigger — to execute my excruciating pain. My abdomen was a scabbard — the home of blades that pierced within me. The man with the bullet was my escape, my relief. He visited my mind when I was completely bent to one side of the bed — the comfortable spot usually in the fetal position — where the pain softens for a mild moment. I did not dare to move.

Migraine vigorously pounded my head. Diarrhea, nausea, fever, and cramps were some of the symptoms I endured. Sometimes the pangs of pain slept idly like a dormant volcano and other times they erupted capriciously. I never thought it was serious. My condition was alien to me and my parents. I blamed it on stress and depression. Naturally, the torture progressed until it exploded on my fragile body like cluster of paint splashed on white canvas. I could no longer hide my distress beneath strong smiles. Spasms of pain punctured my bones. For the first time, I was immobile. I could neither bath, nor change my cloths. I also had trouble swallowing water and food, but the worst part was digesting the truth: I was really ill. I was frustrated that I was losing my independence. Tears welled from my eyes, yet not a sob could be heard. At the age of nineteen, my patience was wearing thin. My parents finally booked a flight to Switzerland. We would seek medical aid from a doctor they trusted and discover what was wrong with me.

We reached Switzerland in a chilled November afternoon. The weather seemed understanding of my situation, as torrential rain accommodated my mood quite agreeably. At night, I tossed and turned on my bed. The nurses with their vampire needles terrified sleep away.

The next day, the nurse gently pricked my goose flesh for blood tests. As I closed my eyes in terror, I noticed that the pain endured was miniscule compared to my huge fear of needles. The doctor called at night and told us I had a virus and an inflammation in my stomach. At least I learned that I did not hallucinate my suffering. It actually had a name!

My weak state compelled me to enroll in a Distance Learning Law Program in Nottingham University. Although I missed university life so much, deep down I knew I was fortunate to learn from home — even if I had to teach myself. I never expected I would miss all the simple things in attending a university the most: strolling to campus, staring out the windows in class, drawing swirls on the margins of my notebook, writing notes till my pen dries out and making new friends every day. It was a shame that I did not value the little things in life until I lost them, but it was no time to count my losses. I had to look at my blessings in the eye and fight for them. It was my only hope to succeed — even if they were blessings in disguise. I felt like they were playing hide-and-seek with me. I was determined to win by seeking each one of them, highlight their significance, and the impact they imprinted on me. They would aid me in weaker times. We would combat future storms together.

With every test tube filled, my fear of needles slowly diminished. The tests confirmed that my hemoglobin was below average. Not only were my emotions suffocated, but also oxygen in my blood aspired to breathe. My soul shriveled with anxiety. I filled the gaps of fear from the unknown with writing — my escape route. Notes on my diary — the friend that never left me — reminded me consistently to stay strong, accept myself, and smile.

At last, I met the specialist — my doctor. He was still uncertain about the type of disease I carried. Further tests and scans would determine the result. I was obliged to drink two liters of the most acrid and bile solution ever. Its pungent odor enveloped my nose. The lemon — my father squeezed inside the mixture — did not make it better. I spent the whole night and morning vomiting.

In the clinic, the specialist performed an 'endoscopy.' He injected deep inside my vein and attached an antiseptic tape to sedate the pain. Camera wires were attached inside my body to scan my colon and terminal ileum. I rested on the bed, cold and exposed. My eyes rained teardrops. My doctor wiped the trails away. "I understand," he told me — fighting his own tears — "you're ashamed. It's fine. You're not alone." This stranger of a doctor felt my real sorrows. He understood the significance of moral therapy before physical treatment – a crucial point which a lot of doctors from diverse nations neglected. Then, I underwent a 'biopsy.' The gastroenterologist took samples of the scattered, spotty patches of inflammation for laboratory analysis.

The specialist told me that inflammation colonized my colon and the border of my intestine. I was finally diagnosed with Crohn's disease. Being told I had a disease that caused great pain was bad enough, but it was something else entirely to be told that it had no cure and I should be under medication for the rest of my life. With the scissors of optimism, I decided to cut the strings of anxiety and stress. In my mind, Crohn's disease was reduced to a stilled puppet, lurking around lifeless. I learned to deal with pressure without internalizing it, so it wouldn't consume me. I became more compassionate and understanding of people's shortcomings, since exhaustion completely drained my energy. I began to look forward to my doctor appointments with my father always by my side. The pinkish-purple souvenir on my arm — courtesy of the needles — was mere proof of the good times my dad and I spent together.

I secretly feared that I might not be able to get pregnant in future or if I was blessed with children, I would not have the energy to care for them. After two years, my fear was kept at rest. I got married and pregnant. In my sixth month, I was mistakenly admitted to the hospital for labor, since Crohn's disease crippling pain greatly resembled contractions. I witnessed a flare-up, because I failed to take my pills. Since then, I promised myself to take my medicine, no matter how much I grew sick of them. With the help of God, family, friends, and medicine, I was battling my disease victoriously. At least it was great practice for giving birth with no epidural or drug to tranquilize the pain. I was reticent through the whole labor experience. It made my gynecologist see girls from the new generation — my generation — in a new light.

Some people chose to dwell on their sufferings and all the miseries a disease entailed. I chose to appreciate all the qualities I acquired after I was diagnosed with Crohn's disease. I was no longer frightened of needles, my writing improved and was very therapeutic, as it provided me with the perfect outlet to unleash any negative energy on paper, and I became more sympathetic and closer to family and friends, especially my father. But most importantly, all the suffering ignited my soul with hope. I looked at my disease as a windowpane in a winter morning — snow filtering the glass from flaws, blemishes, and scars of the years. I felt purified — closer to God than ever before. Before my son turns six, I held three more children in my arms. I no longer felt incapable to raise them.

The man with the gun had waved his final goodbye. I got my miracle.

SOMETHING HOLY
By Cherise Wyneken

Two-hour surgery, lasted six.
Two-night stay – two months.
Complications snowballed
like dust motes without a ray of sun.
Multi-system organ failure.
No chance with surgery, but they'll try.

Terror snatched me from my robin's nest,
grabbed my throat with its beak, and squeezed
my breath away like water from a sponge.
Prayers flew up from many faiths
to the god they knew. Doubt crept in behind
and seesawed in my echo chamber.

Next week – same scene.
No time to stop the gurney, grinding toward OR,
for me to give a good-bye kiss.
Tubes in his side for nourishment,
tubes in his throat for air,
tubes to his veins recycling blood.
> *We are together in this room –*
> *a walled-in box, filled with monitors*
> *and IV bags dripping blue solution.*
> *We are together in this room,*
> *yet we are far apart.*
> *I cannot see inside your head.*
> *I cannot hear your thoughts.*
> *Your voice is trapped within.*
> *I am here beside you – alone.*

May crept into June.
July brought plans for a nursing home
readied with a respirator – possibly for life.
Certain he could manage without machines,

refusing to give up, Nurse Debby
disconnects the oxygen, watches as he breathes.
Three weeks later, unplugged, learning to use his legs,
able to swallow soup and applesauce,
I brought the car around for a man alive.

PROTECT ME
By Jean Varda

Protect me from his shouting
from his angry eyes and sweaty
hands. Cover me with kindness
that does not yell and hurt,
shelter me with flowers
with dry leaves and grass.
Lie down next to me,
hold me, asking nothing from me
just the quietness of kindness,
the sweetness of your words.

IN THE RADIATION THERAPY ROOM
By Lucinda Grey

I open the door to the Caribbean,
pass murals of the sea, take off
my sandals and stretch out on a table
for a massage in Cancun. I slip off
my gown to lie topless, expectant
in green laser light. My breast tattooed
in purple and gold Magic Markers,
shimmers iridescent as a neon fish
flashing through turquoise waters.
After the healing beams of the sun
penetrate my breast, I arise changed,
to walk past the sea, back
to my landlocked life.

JENNIFER
By Deborah Lamkin Smith

Precious gift of God. That's what was hand embroidered on the top of a mason jar I received as a gift when Jennifer was born. The 18 years I had with her was indeed a gift from God. Jennifer Brook Lamkin, my only child, was born on August 25th, 1980. Even as a toddler she seemed wise beyond her years. She loved to read and write and had a talent for expressing herself in her journals and poems. She won a poetry contest when she was in the 4th grade out of over 200 students. Little did I know that only 9 months after she wrote "I Want to See God" that she would go to be with God.

I'll never forget the day she showed me her poem. She told me she'd had a hard time going to sleep the night before. So she started thinking about heaven and what it would be like to see God. She soon fell asleep and the next morning she regretted not writing down the things she had thought about. She told me "I prayed that I could remember, so I took a pencil and paper and it all seemed like it flowed through my hand just like I remembered it!"

I WANT TO SEE GOD
By Jennifer Brook Lamkin

I want to see God. I know that I will one day but that's <u>after</u> I die. I want to see Him here and now-- His greatness against the dull comparison of this world. Why can't I see Him now? What rule is there? Would it cause me to become jealous of His beauty? Blinded by the light? Overwhelmed by the greatness? Would it cause me to become bored of this world? If I saw His beauty, would I not care to see anything else? Would the wonderful landscapes of this earth become plain and insignificant?

If we saw God, His light would make the sun seem dim. His color would be a color we never knew existed on the spectrum. His eyes so intense with love, they would seem to burn with the fire of all the years He has known us. His voice would be so much louder than thunder...but sweeter than the voices of all the angels together. And all of this is just the outward appearance. His love for us would be so strong in our presence that we would be able to see it, hear it, smell it, and even taste it in the air. Its thickness would probably suffocate us, if it weren't for the extreme gentleness of His ways. His hands have the strength of all the universe. He has molded the planets, the galaxies, the mountains and all the same He has made the tiniest creature...and each grain of sand, and each leaf on the trees, and each hair on our heads. He knows every thought we think whether we know we thought it or not.

I pity anyone who doesn't believe in such an awesome and wonderful concept. What could be any better than having someone so great as a Father?

She read this poem on youth talent night at our church. Copies were given to everyone who attended her funeral. It has also gone as far as Russia through the youth ministry. I've shared it with many people I met while working in the hospital who were going through grief or illness.

Sharing her writings with others has helped me to heal over the years. I know one day she'll welcome me into heaven and show me all the glorious things God revealed to her that night.

JUST IN TIME
By Sharon Fulham

Never underestimate the power of a small kindness. It was an ordinary day at the family restaurant where I worked in Northern California in 1966. I was twenty-one and this was my first job. I loved the fast pace of restaurant work and the friendly environment. After the lunch rush and in between serving customers I mentioned to a co-worker that I was going to the hospital after work to visit a close friend who had surgery. Emily, the morning cook overheard my comment. "Oh, Sharon if you don't mind, would you drop by to visit my mom? She broke her leg the other day and I can't see her until later this evening. Mom could sure use the company." I assured her that I would stop in to visit her mother whose name was Pearl. I had never met her before.

Later, after spending ample time with my friend who had surgery, I hurried down the hall to meet Emily's mother, Pearl. With an inspirational magazine in hand that I grabbed from my car, I stepped into her room. When I introduced myself as her daughter's friend from the restaurant she smiled warmly. I was grateful I had come. Pearl appeared to be around sixty years of age. Glancing at her cast I asked how she was feeling. She was comfortable and looked forward to going home. She appreciated the magazine and looked forward to reading it soon. The subject of Heaven came up in our conversation which led to an experience she had years ago during a very serious surgery. She believed she had died and gone to a place she believed to be Heaven. She was convinced this was not a dream or vision. Pearl certainly had my undivided attention!

"Oh, it was just beautiful," she wooed as if seeing this place all over again.... She spoke of the lush green trees and how they flourished everywhere... The air was fresh and clean and the light was brighter than daylight on earth. She spoke of the bountiful flowers, and their vibrant colors and sweet fragrances. The grass was vividly green and there were birds chirping all around... She was happy there. Her smile widened when she spoke of the wonderful peace she experienced. Nothing on earth could compare to the peace. It seemed she had been in Heaven a long time. She preferred to stay but it was not meant to be. I stood there awestruck and speechless... right? I never expected to hear this. I knew this experience was her reality ... and quite believable to me. "Pearl," I spoke softly, "I believe in a place called Heaven and it sounds to me like you were there." Her peaceful eyes met mine and she smiled in agreement. It seemed time stood still as she relived her story. As I drove home my heart was light with joy as I pondered Pearl's amazing experience....

The next morning at work I noticed that Emily was not there. I sadly discovered that her mother passed away during the night. A blood clot had traveled from her broken leg to her heart. I was shocked to my core. It seemed I had just left her hospital room. Emily was to come in after lunch to pick up her paycheck. Shaken, my stomach began to churn. I took an early break to write down what I remembered of her dream. When Emily arrived at the restaurant I embraced her offering my condolences. She wept. "I didn't expect my mother to die from a broken leg. What am I going to do without her? Where is she now? I want my mother." My heart ached for her...

I took Emily aside privately and told her the beautiful experience her mother shared with me. She was not aware of her mother's realistic dream about a place she believed to be Heaven... She had never heard of this. Eagerly she listened to every word and detail as if picturing her mother in this beautiful place. I looked at her with heartfelt compassion and sincerity. "I believe your mother is at peace Emily, just like she explained in her dream. She is happy now." Tears of relief trickled down her cheeks and warmed her smile. I choked up.... With voice breaking I handed her my handwritten copy of her mother's realistic dream. "This is for you Emily" ... She held it against her heart with both hands ... tear-filled eyes looking into mine. Emily was comforted with her mother's own words.

A calming peace settled over me as I realized that I became a part of God's timing in the life of Emily and her mother. I was humbled ... A small favor forever changed my thinking. There are no accidents. A small act of kindness can easily turn into something much larger. Kindness cannot be measured. If I had not said that I was going to the hospital to visit a friend, Emily would never have asked me to visit her mother whom I didn't know was even there. When Pearl shared her dream about Heaven I had no idea that her words would comfort her grieving daughter the next day.

Never underestimate the power of a kind action. When an opportunity presents itself to make a human being's life better... take it. I cherish these words.... "Do unto others as you would have them do unto you."

FIGHTING INERTIA
By Susan Mahan

You have died and left me.
For a time, I long to be with you,
to burrow down and cover us both with dirt.
But, let me go forth.
There is nothing else I can do.
I will hold on to my sanity with measured steps.

I have never been alone,
and I am filled with fear,
but let me go forth.
I will somehow seek solace
in the sound of one heart beating.

I do not have the strength
to go on without you,
but let me go forth.
I will take strength from our shared memories
while I build my own.

I so miss what we had.
It will be a long, long life without you,
but I will put one foot
in front of the other,
and I will go forth.

MIRACLE
By Lynn C. Johnston

If you had asked me five years ago what road my life would take, I never could have anticipated most of the events that occurred. During this period, my always healthy mother was diagnosed with pancreatic cancer and succumbed to the disease seven months later. I was laid off from my job two months after the funeral. The next few years didn't get any better with only temporary job prospects and deepening financial woes.

I thought I had pretty much hit rock bottom. Then in the fall of 2009, my precious indoor Calico cat, Valentine, got outside and vanished.

Feeling like my nightmare was only getting worse, I was tormented with visions of all the horrible things she could encounter. Had she been injured by another animal or a car? Was she being held against her will? Was she getting enough food?

I plastered the neighborhood with flyers and knocked on nearly every door, meeting most of my neighbors for the first time. As I showed them her picture, their faces fell, often recalling their own agony of a lost pet. I asked that if they were religiously inclined to please keep Valentine's safe return in their prayers.

My teenage son and I roamed the neighborhood every night with flashlights, just hoping to catch a glimpse of her. And each night when we returned home unsuccessful, I was heartbroken. As the days dragged on, my hopes and faith were fading. I was crushed. It seemed as if God was kicking me when I was down.

But one night, three weeks to the day after she disappeared, my son announced that he heard her collar bell ringing outside. My heart leapt.

"Are you sure?" I said, too afraid to have my hopes dashed again.

"Yes, and I saw her. It was dark, but I'm sure it was her." He went on to say that she ran into the yard of the apartment building next door.

When he said that, I spontaneously broke into tears. I couldn't stop crying. She wasn't home yet, but at least I knew she was alive and healthy enough to run.

The next day we rented a humane animal trap from our local shelter, filled it with small chucks of Kentucky Fried Chicken (as they recommended), and prayed for a miracle. I slept on the living room sofa so I could be near our front door if the trap closed.

At three o'clock in the morning, my prayers were answered. Valentine was in the trap, filthy, scared, and about three pounds lighter than she left. I was never so happy to see her in my life.

I dropped to my knees and thanked God for bringing her home safely and bringing her light back into my life. It was a miracle.

That night, though Valentine, I learned two valuable lessons that have helped sustain me in times of crisis ever since: Miracles do happen and nightmares can have happy endings.

JAIL: FREE
By Joy Case, M. Ed

my heart bruises on these bars
set laden with care for not
I am here.
Entrapped soul with weary eyes;
I lie crippled by weight
that I didn't create.
Bones brittle. Flesh withering...
Not the plans I made.
Life lived in the shade.
The ache keeps me awake
Time slowly marching...
It's hard to Breathe in here.
I'm LOVE. I'm LIGHT.
Get out of this dark night.
Still I lay beyond earth, I pray
is more for this Creation that now lays waste to Not.
I feel Not. Here.
Not there. Not ready. Not...
Out of this jail I break free for the glory that might befall!
Souls shine; I transcend these bends.
But not broken I Return to the Garden.
Free

BUTTERFLY
By Alina Zeng

Face flushing, hair free in wind,
I trudge toward the frost-glazed lake.
Snide comments muttered in the halls
Echo in my mind and turn to shouts.
I inch further to the heart of the ice;
Peering into patches of water, I
See what I don't want to see:
My birthmark on my left cheek
Reflects back at me. I hurt more.
Then my eyes flicker to my wrist
Where a frayed bracelet peeks out
From my sweater. I tug it off,
Remember my sister's gentle hands
Tying the knot that has held to now:
Her gift, despite my self-hatred
Often forcing me to take my blade
And cut my arm where no one
Would ever see, not even she.
I remember her tracing my blotch,
Whisper it was like a butterfly--
As I ached for it to fly off my face
To some garden where it belonged.
Still, thinking of her kindness
Makes the nasty voices fade away
Until I can hear my own voice
Comforting me like my sister did
Long ago. One step too far and the
Ice cracks, pulling me through as
Numbness rushes into my veins;
But I clench the bracelet, grab
The slippery ledge, pull myself up
Breathing in self-acceptance, and
Head home where my sister waits.

TO THOMAS
By Carolyn T. Johnson

Impact statements given by plaintiffs at the end of a criminal case didn't exist back in the late 70's, when you were on trial. The court didn't allow me, or the other nine women you tried to strangle, to address you at the end of the trial to tell you what impact your crime had on our lives.

There wasn't a Victims Services Division to notify us when you were paroled from prison after serving only 8 years of your 123-year sentence. No one informed us when you were re-arrested for the same crimes nor told us when you died of AIDS in prison.

No, we victims of violent crime did not have a voice back then, but we do now.

It's too late for me because you're now six feet under, buried in a Veteran's Cemetery in the same town where I now live. But, I'm moved to write you this letter, one that you will never see, but one that others might. Your impact still lingers with me. Especially when Memorial Day rolls around and my anger bubbles up yet again, knowing you share common ground with our fallen heroes.

I bet you weren't aware that I was considered one of the lucky ones. Rather than you hiding in my apartment until I fell fast asleep, like you did with the other women you attacked; you planned on sneaking up behind me on the living room couch and wrapping your necktie around my neck. But I accidentally found you first, behind the bedroom door, and I fought back. It felt good knowing I'd tried to punch you in the crotch then scrape my long pointy fingernails down your cheeks. If my arms had only been a little longer, I would have tried to tear your eyeballs right out of their sockets.

Did you know it only takes three minutes of restricted blood flow to the brain to cause irreparable damage? Were you thinking about that while you were on top of my shins strangling me?

When your necktie ripped in half and my legs unfolded, I sent you flying. I bet you were shocked and maybe even embarrassed – a young petite woman throwing a grown man against a wall like that. Then you panicked and ran out. You had no idea that I'd grabbed a pair of scissors off the kitchen counter and had run after you, wanting to stab you in the back, at least until I came to my senses.

I was angry because I couldn't identify you in the police lineup, but without your menacing black knit ski cap pulled down low over your forehead, I didn't recognize you. I was one of the few who actually saw you with the light on, but I could only narrow it down to two of you.

Do you remember looking up at me and smiling when I took the stand during your trial? I sure do. My heart pounded in my ears as the judge swore me in. The district attorney told me not to look your direction, but I couldn't help myself. I hadn't laid eyes on you since that night you threw me down on the bed and wrapped your necktie around my neck. My heart quickens even now when I think about fighting for breath.

Did you know that some serial killers start out as Peeping Toms, progress to assault and rape and, eventually, when the thrill of domination isn't enough, murder? Sounds familiar, doesn't it? But you got caught before you killed one of us. Or were we just fortunate that you didn't?

I was elated when you were finally apprehended, convicted, and thrown in jail. I went on with my life, content that your fellow prisoners would not be too happy with a bunkmate who picked on women.

I feel better having shared in writing your impact on me. I've become much more aware of my surroundings, listen carefully to my sixth sense, and never ever wear tight turtlenecks. But I've had a profound impact on you too. Rather than going down in history as a famous, sadistic controlling villain, you'll always be known as a weak, cowardly, pathetic nobody.

REBOUND
By Theresa M. Leslie

From the kitchen, I hear the ball
Bouncing in the driveway
And then our children pound,
Bound downstairs, brother and
Sister laughing, taunting as they slam
Outdoors in a race for their dad
And a game of basketball. I stand
Watching from the window, and
Remember our family of five —
Now four.

Summer evenings, dinner almost
Finished, my husband carried
His plate to the sink, snuck outside,
And the bouncing began.
All three children shoveled last bites
Into mouths begging to be excused,
My answer always *Yes!* Dinner dishes
Forgotten we flew to play basketball,
Sometimes girls against boys,
Sometimes parents against kids.

Ever, our youngest slowed the game,
Stopped with the ball, thought long
Where to pass. Teasing, the rest of us
Called her Statue--to Abby's chagrin.
Still, shouting and whooping, we five
Played until it got too dark to see.

But unforeseen, she left the team,
Went to play with the angels
In a more patient world than ours.
Often I wondered how to survive
But the answer came slowly.
Today, I rush out the door
To join them as I used to do,
Her spirit encircling us
As we play.

FOR BETTER, FOR WORSE
By Lisa Braxton

I turned away from the hospital monitor because I was distressed by what I was seeing. On one side of the screen was an image of my left kidney, a bright, bean-shaped silhouette. But on the other side was a picture of my right kidney, a smaller, shapeless smudge, dimly lit. I'd come to the hospital for a renal scan to measure my kidney function after a routine physical indicated that something was wrong. Now I lay on a scanning table hooked to an I.V. that sent a radioactive dye through my veins. A special camera took pictures of the dye in my kidneys.

The procedure can make patients feel chilled. When the radiology technician came into the room to see if I wanted another blanket, I asked her what the smudge on the screen meant. Maintaining an upbeat tone of voice, she told me I'd have to wait until I talked to my doctor.

I didn't have to. I could see that my right kidney was severely damaged. That night after I left the hospital I prayed, *Dear Lord, please bring my right kidney back to life. Please lead me to some medicine that will make it normal again.*

In the months before my physical I had been jubilant. I had gotten engaged to Alex, a man I met in church, and was planning the wedding of my dreams at a mansion rented to the public for special occasions. I was looking forward to a new and exciting chapter in my life. I refused to believe that something was wrong with the kidney. I thought the renal scan would confirm that an error was made in the initial lab test results.

Several days after the test at the hospital I went to see the urologist who ordered it. "I'm sorry, Lisa, your right kidney has a blockage. There's not much function at all," he said. "But on the bright side, your left kidney is working as it should. Many people go through a lifetime with only one kidney."

He asked me if I wanted to talk to a kidney specialist to try to determine why I had the blockage. I said that I did. Alex squeezed my hand as we left the doctor's office. "I'm sorry this is happening to you," he said.

"Many people go through a lifetime with only one kidney." I kept the doctor's words in the back of my mind in the weeks leading up to the appointment with the nephrologist, spending my evenings working on a seating chart for my wedding reception and sifting through CDs of wedding music to find the song I wanted played when I marched down the aisle.

My determination to remain strong began to dissolve when the nephrologist came into the examining room for our appointment. "There may be something wrong with your functioning kidney," he said, looking over my blood work. "We'll have to do more tests."

I was devastated. I was putting all of my hopes into the remaining kidney. If something was wrong with that one, what kind of quality of life would I have? What kind of partner would I be to Alex?

"Will I have to go on dialysis?" I asked.

"Let's not get ahead of ourselves," the doctor said. "The tests should tell us what's going on."

I had spent much of my adult life focused on my career as a television news reporter and anchor, wanting to work my way up to a major television market. I moved to a different station in a different part of the country every few years to strengthen my experience. This made dating difficult. When I decided to leave television and settled in one place, I prayed for a husband to share my life with. For years, no one who seemed right for me came along. I accepted what I thought was God's plan.

Then, when I was in my late 40s, I met Alex. We were in the same adult Sunday school class at our church for years but never spoke until Alex, who was divorced, felt ready to begin dating again. During our courtship we discovered a shared interest in watching old sitcoms and movies from the 1970s that were popular when we were kids. Avid readers, we'd trade magazines and books and then have discussions about them. After Sunday church services we'd have lively discussions about the pastor's sermon. Six months after we began dating we knew we wanted to get married.

Early in our relationship I told Alex about an emergency surgery I'd had years before we met to correct damage done during a previous surgery that took away all hope I had of ever having a child. I now suspected that the stents put in place to help me heal, ended up causing damage, leading to a gradual but steady blockage to my right kidney.

After hearing what the nephrologist had to say that day, I didn't feel comfortable involving Alex any further with my problems. He had a teenage daughter who would soon start college. He didn't need to be burdened with a disabled wife who'd have mounting medical bills. I thought I should let him out of the engagement. I prayed, asking God if I was making the right decision.

Unable to sleep that night I sent an email to my pastor asking for prayer to help me cope with my medical problems and the decision I felt I had to make about Alex.

The following Sunday as I sat in the pew reading the church bulletin before service began, I was surprised to hear my name called. The pastor asked me to come to the altar. The ministerial staff, in their vestments and clergy robes, came down from the pulpit and surrounded me. The congregation joined in the prayer. After the church service, the pastor emeritus, who'd had his own recent medical struggles, pulled me aside, gave me a hug, and said he would be praying for me.

The outpouring of love I received gave me the strength to face my upcoming appointment with the nephrologist and to have the conversation with Alex. When I tried to tell him that he didn't have to marry me, he wouldn't even let me get to the end of my sentence.

"Leaving you never even crossed my mind," he said.

Alex was at my side at the next appointment when the doctor gave me the results of the additional tests. The doctor said that what he saw in my blood work should not be harmful and that the remaining kidney was functioning fine. But I'd have to watch it closely. I'd have to come back periodically to have the kidney monitored.

Alex and I walked out of the doctor's office relieved at the news. I looked up at him and couldn't help but smile. This was the man who made a commitment to me the day he put a ring on my finger, but showed me the depth of that commitment when I needed it most.

AFTER THE HURRICANE
By Mary Laufer

Our neighbors drove inland
or evacuated to safe shelters
before the monster storm hit.
They returned the next day and found
pine trees lying on top of their houses,
exposed rafters, and collapsed walls.
Their belongings were scattered
all over the neighborhood.
They cried long and hard,
raised their arms into the air,
and asked God, "Why us?"

We took refuge in our bathroom that night,
listened to the howling wind for seven hours,
shuddered at each boom and bang,
and prayed fervently to Heaven
that our family be kept from harm.
In the morning, we stepped outside
and found pine trees lying on top of our house,
exposed rafters, and collapsed walls.
Our belongings were scattered
all over the neighborhood.

We hugged each other,
proclaimed it a miracle that no one was hurt,
then raised our arms into the air
and thanked God we were still alive.

LOST BUT NOT ALONE
By Ruth E. Smith

My name is Ruth, and my journey with the Lord started in a little town called Dearing, Georgia, in 1971. I lived in a small mobile home park.

It was a dark and lonely night, and the stars were shining brightly. I had two daughters who were asleep in their beds. My husband who had a drinking problem was away for a couple of weeks, where I did not know. I had no friends. I felt lost, lonely, rejected and unloved. I was at the end on my rope about to let go. I had been depressed for quite a while. Not thinking at the time, even of my two young daughters, I could see no reason for living. To me it seemed one was born, struggled through life and then died, end of story.

In my grief, I went outside and looked up at the stars crying and I prayed, "If there is a God and You really have a purpose for me being here, please show me. If God you are real I want to know the truth, the whole truth and nothing but the truth about you and life. So Help Me God Please, I need to know."

I was not one who went to church nor did I read the Bible. It was only a couple of days later I heard in my spirit, as I stood in the living room of my trailer, "Go get that Bible you have in your dresser drawer, that your grandmother gave you, that you have never read, and read it." It was strange I did not question what I heard; I just went and got it. I heard these words within me say "Everything you want to know about life can be found there." I read and read. The more I read, the more I wanted to read.

The next morning when I walked down the road to the mailbox, I felt like I was floating on clouds. All I could think about was I am a child of GOD. I could hardly contain my joy.

I did not want to stop reading. I know now it was the Holy Spirit teaching me about God's Word. I knew there was someone who loved me and had come to save me from the meaningless life I was living. His Word said, "Do not fear, for I am with you; do not be dismayed, for I am your God. I will strengthen you and help you. For everyone who asks it will be given to them, and because you asked you will find the road that leads to life. Jesus said therefore, everyone who hears these words of mine and puts them into practice is like a wise man who built his house on the rock. The rain came down, the streams rose, and the winds blew and beat against that house; yet it did not fall, because it had it foundation on the rock."

I learned how Jesus came into the world to teach us how to overcome in this life and give us a purpose to live. He said to me in His Word, "You don't understand now why you had to go through what you have, but you will. I Am the Light of the World. Whoever follows Me will never walk in darkness, but will have the light of life. Whoever finds Me finds life and receives favor from the Lord. And they that know My name will put their trust in Me, for I the Lord have not forsaken them that seek Me."

I prayed, "May the words of my mouth and the meditation of my heart would be pleasing to You, O Lord. Show me your ways, teach me your paths."

A week later I wrote to my grandmother and told her I was reading the Bible she gave me, and what it meant to me. She sent me a postcard and told me she hoped I would get into a church soon. I didn't know where to go to church or how to get there, since I had no transportation.

The day after I received the postcard, a preacher and two members from the Baptist congregation in Dearing came to visit me one evening. I was so excited to see them; I hardly gave them time to get in the door. I told them all about how I was reading the Bible and what I was learning. They had come to invite me to church. I told them I would come but I had no way of getting there. The preacher said he could come and get me and my children.

It was near Easter when I went to the preacher and asked him about me being baptized. He said he could baptize me by immersion on Easter Sunday.

I stayed at this church until my husband got a new job in Atlanta, GA. The preacher and his wife encouraged me to visit Woodland Hills Baptist Church, in Atlanta, where some of their friends attended. Not long after, we moved to Orlando, Florida.

I know God's Word is true, as I have come to understand it. It says faith comes from hearing the word of Christ, and that's how I learned there was a God. "Draw near to God and He will draw near to you."

I will never ever forget the night I came to know the Lord; the one who accepted me just as I was unknowing, full of doubts, questioning, but seeking to know the truth.

It is amazing how God comes into our life, when we call out to Him. I am very blessed! I have learned so much about life and am continuing to learn. Because of all that I have been through, I have so much compassion for those who have not yet come to have a personal relationship with the Lord.

I do attend church, but do not see myself as belonging to a certain type of faith or religion. I see myself as belonging to the family of God, which includes people of all walks of life wherever they may be.

I now am member of the most wonderful church I have ever attended, Windermere Union Church of Christ, in Windermere, Florida. The church is like none I have ever been to before. You can feel the presence of the Lord there when you walk through the door. The people love the Lord. They are the friendliest, most compassionate, understanding, accepting, and giving people you would ever want to meet. They love you for who you are, no matter where you are in your journey of life.

Jesus said, in his word, "If you hold to my teaching, you are really my disciples. Then you will know the truth, and the truth will set you free. I have told you these things, so that in me you may have peace. In this world you will have trouble. But take heart! I have overcome the world. I am the way the truth and the life."

I know God heard my prayer, the night that I called out to Him, and my life has never been the same. I do not know what God plans are for me in the future, but I know it's a life of purpose, just like I asked Him for, a reason for living.

SOMETHING DID SURVIVE
By Lynn C. Johnston

With a fury loud as thunder
Our world was torn apart
Hurling chards of broken dreams flew out
From our shattered hearts
But you weren't just a lover
You were also my best friend
Until that fateful day arrived
When it all came to an end
I couldn't cry upon your shoulder
Or lay in your arms until dawn
For when I lost your love I knew
Our friendship, too, was gone
So many times I thought of you
And longed to hear your voice
To ask how things were going
But I felt I had no choice
No choice because our friendship perished
With the love we shared
That was until I saw your face
And learned we both still cared
You had felt the same way
And you, too, missed your best friend
As we talked and listened,
We felt our hearts begin to mend
Amidst the pain and heartbreak
We learned something did survive
Although it wasn't quite the same
Our friendship was alive

MY JOURNEY OUT OF DARKNESS INTO LIGHT
By R. Todd La Flame

When I was born in December 1963, I was completely blind. My eyes had filled with blood due to being born a month early and a difficult delivery. At eight weeks old, I was to have surgery to remove both of my eyes and to receive glass ones. While on the operating table, the blood started to dissolve. When the doctors emerged from the operating room crying, my mom thought I had died. They told her that I could see. I believe God has had a hand on me because of this miracle.

My mother had polio at the age of seven and was confined to a wheelchair. When I was born, her family wanted to take me away from her to give me to one of her sisters to raise. They did not believe she could take care of a baby, especially one who was legally blind. Determined to prove them wrong, she moved out, got a job, and learned how to drive a car, all while raising me on her own. When I was seven she married a man who, through both physical & verbal abuse, convinced me that I was worthless. Finally, when I was 14, they divorced.

It was at that time, I found a large charismatic church though a neighbor. During the service the pastor began to call out people in the congregation by the Spirit of God. I was one of those people. When the pastor asked me if I was saved, I said yes. Then he asked me if I had received the Holy Spirit. I said no, and he then laid hands on me and I began to speak in tongues.

I also started to realize that I was different. I was noticing boys when I should have been noticing girls. I learned that this meant I was gay. At church they said that a person like me was demon posed and going to hell. The only way to fix this was to have the demon cast out of me. So, starting at the age of about 15, I began to go through exorcisms. These lasted anywhere from an hour to four or five hours. I would throw myself into a frenzy, hyperventilate to the point of not being able to breath and then vomiting. It would be declared that the demon had left and I was set free from the sin of homosexuality. Within a week or two the feelings would come back when I would notice a good looking man that walked by or was on TV. I would go back to my spiritual leaders and they would say I had let the demon back in. So the whole process would start over again.

This went on for the next five to six years of my life. There were many times that I thought about killing myself to set me free from my struggle. In junior high I met a young girl and we became best friends. We started dating in high school, and before I left for college I decided to ask her to marry me. I figured if I got married than that would fix me; God would give me the "correct" feelings before the wedding.

After a year of being engaged nothing changed for me. Two weeks before my wedding I told her I could not marry her because it would ruin her life and mine. I would be living a lie, and I just could not do that to either one of us.

One Sunday my pastor said that the only way to get a gay person into Heaven was to have them come down front, kneel down, and say the Sinners Prayer. Then you should shoot them in the back of the head before they got up. He was not joking. I got up and walked out and vowed to never return to church. God did not want me and His people certainly didn't.

After my mom passed away at age 48, I began searching for the love I so longed for. Over the next several years, I became a heavy drinker, visiting bars at least two or three times a week. I filled my life with sex and drinking. If a new man showed up at the bar it became my job to find a way to go to bed with him.

Then I met Glenn. I met the man that I knew loved me no matter what. It didn't matter that I might lose my vision one day, he loved me. I was slowly going totally blind, due to cataracts, from all of the surgeries that I had during my life.

With the love of my partner, I began to search for a more meaningful spiritual life. A year and a half after getting together, Glenn was diagnosed with AIDS and I was told I was HIV positive. We found a place that offered holistic healing and it started me thinking about my relationship to God.

One evening while watching TV, a commercial came on with these two bouncers out in front of a church. "No, you're not welcome." My God, he was talking to me! "Jesus didn't turn people away and neither do we. The United Church of Christ."

They don't mean that, I thought. They just want to get you in the door and then they will make you change. It went on, "no matter who you are or where you are on life's journey. You are welcomed here."

Really? Not me. Not an openly gay, HIV-positive man who God's people have rejected. But was it possible? I called the church, St. Luke's UCC in Northeast Philadelphia, and spoke to a woman, telling her that I wanted to come to church but I had some questions.

"I am gay, is that ok?"

"Yes," she said, "that is fine."

"I am HIV-positive and I am very vocal about it. I don't want people to be running when I come down to take communion. Is that ok?"

"Yes, that is fine," she said again.

"Now for the next one, I don't drive and I need a ride to church, can someone come and pick me up for church?" She assured me that someone could get me.

Two weeks later, I walked into St. Luke's and it was as if I had come home. The pastor, Chris Paules, would teach me to see God in a new and amazing way. God loved me and had even CREATED ME the way I was, and loved me more than I could ever imagine. I went home that Sunday and called several of my friends and told them, "YOU'RE NOT GOING TO BELIEVE THIS CHURCH I FOUND!"

Over time, I began to share my story of love & acceptance with others, in hopes that they would not have to go through the fear and rejection I had as a young man.

Now living in Florida, my life is fuller than I could ever imagine. I am a part of a thriving and growing church, Windermere Union Church UCC in Windermere, Florida, led by Pastor Barton Buchanan. The people of WUC have been so welcoming and have continued to help me to grow in my walk with God. In August of 2013, Glenn and I were married. The entire church jumped in and helped us with everything we needed. From tuxes to a cake, it was all taken care of by our friends from WUC, who we consider family.

We could not feel more supported. I am now head of the Warm Welcome Team at WUC. We make sure that first time visitors know that no matter what, they are welcomed in our church. We also facilitate those who want to become new member of the church.

Glenn & I now live in Ocoee, Florida, with our dog Bandit. We have been together for almost 19 years, married for almost 3. We are both healthy and looking forward to the future. I am also now a Stephen Minister, which means I have gone through 50 hours of training to learn how to help those going through life changing events. I am no longer worried about people running out of the church when I come down to take communion, in fact, I have even been called to help serve communion on several occasions.

So this is my story. I share it in hopes of letting other LGBT people know that they can find a spiritual home in the UCC. This is a place where we are truly loved and cared for. We are welcomed into all aspects and life within the church. Come here and you can grow and live a life you never thought possible. No matter who you are, or where you are on life's journey. You are welcome here.

SCAR TISSUE
By Carolyne Van Der Meer

When the photographer asked her
if she wanted him to Photoshop
her scars, she was surprised
at the violence of her reaction

There were three:
one at the base of her neck
one near her left clavicle and the third
just above her left breast

Initially, she went silent
There were two levels to the offense:
that he asked her at all and that
their removal should be necessary

What she didn't expect was that
after so many years of wanting them gone
she was now fiercely opposed
to being without them

They sit and look at the photos together
and he tells her
he had to ask her
Part of the job, he says

She looks at him squarely, eyes wet,
tells him she'll no longer hide
Instead she'll wear those scars
with pride

SURVIVING AFTER A MOMENT SHATTERS YOUR WORLD
By Beckie A. Miller

Before October 19, 1991, I was happily married, raising two children, Brian, who had just turned eighteen, and fourteen-year old, Christie. We lived on our horse property surrounded by mountainous deserts in the middle of Phoenix, Arizona. I was also at the time a stay-at-home daycare provider.

My husband Don, and I were married in 1972 and Brian, our firstborn son, was born eleven months later in Rome, New York, where we were stationed at the time as Don was in the Air Force. We moved to Phoenix in December 1975, again due to deployment orders for the military and eventually, loving the area so much, made the valley our permanent home.

The doorbell ringing to the tune of "Hush Little Baby" that fateful October night completely shattered my world. A policeman informed us Brian had been robbed and shot walking his girlfriend home from the bowling alley in our neighborhood. Losing a child to anything is devastating but losing a child to violence transcends to catastrophic. It is the ultimate nightmare a parent will ever face. Our world suddenly made no sense. We were thrust into a scary and confusing judicial process that eventually failed us by allowing the killer of our son to only serve seven-years in prison.

It took us several years to truly begin living again without simply going through the motions. I remember those days I smiled simply because the track lines on my mouth knew how to, but emotionally my smile was broken - disconnected. I cooked meals and tended to my family while questioning how the world dared to keep on going on as if nothing had happened. It took much hard grief work and soul-searching before I could accept my life forever changed by two bullets to my son's chest for his wallet. The first beginning step that guided me on the course of how to rebuild my life happened when I went home the first Christmas after Brian's death.

My mom had asked us to come to Kansas knowing how difficult the holidays were going to be. I agreed, even though I truly did not want to go, simply because the alternative of being in our home without

Brian was worse. On Christmas Eve, I was sitting at mom's kitchen table when the phone rang. It was my brother, Jim, who was in the Navy. I could tell by her end of the conversation that my brother asked her how I was doing. My mom replied, "Pretty good considering she will never get over this." It was as if she had literally slapped me across the face. You see, for the past weeks since Brian was so cruelly taken from me, I had been giving myself time increments for survival. If I could make it through the funeral... If I could make it through Thanksgiving... If I could make it through that first Christmas, I would be okay. This horrific God-awful pain would then end, as I felt I could not possibly continue to live with it. It's an all-consuming pain that drowns you with waves of unimaginable grief. What Mom said to my brother was a shocking wake-up call. However, it made me realize something I could not face until that point. I was never going to get over my son's murder. I ran to the bedroom and cried the entire night, but before dawn that Christmas morning I realized that if I was never going to get over this, as my heart had known all along and my traumatized mind could not accept, then how was I going to live with it?

Part of learning how to go on with life after this moment of revelation happened after that Christmas was when my husband, my daughter, and myself sought help in the support group, Parents of Murdered Children (POMC), for the families and friends of those who have died by violence. Just fifteen-months later I became its leader, somehow instinctively knowing that helping others would allow whatever measure of healing was possible. It gave me a purpose in living with the unending pain and relentless sorrow of my son's loss. Helping others to cope with the aftermath of murder became my mission and a passion that still fuels me nearly twenty-four years later.

Transitioning from daycare mom to leading a group that needed so many things, such as funds, brought me out of my cocoon, and allowed my wings to fly places I never knew I could. I learned to write grants, put on major fund-raisers, host national conferences, do public speaking, and media interviews, facilitate grief retreats, meet with professionals, and ultimately show them how they could better assist crime victims. I learned to go to the legislature and fight for new laws for the rights of crime victims or oppose stupid ones. I also learned while I could hold the hand of our members in need, I could not fix this for them. I could, however, provide them with as much support and information to help them learn about traumatic grief and navigate the confusion and frustrations of the criminal justice system. POMC allows a safe place for our families to vent the emotional pain of what murder leaves behind, and education to allow our members the power to help themselves and to regain some control over their shattered lives.

It was a great struggle at times leaving my protective cocoon and gaining my butterfly wings. I realized somewhere along the journey if God came to me and said I could have my old life back, of course, I would take my son back. I would not, however, want my old life exactly as it was. The lessons and places my wings have taken me in order to give meaning to my son's death are too important to lose.

I have met some of the most courageous people who have been through unspeakable tragedy and they still forge on, unsteadily, and for a long time robotically, but eventually they rebuild and accept a "new normal". They become better people despite tragedy and they make a profound difference in our world.

If I had not survived Brian's loss I would not have experienced the joy of a new child in my life. In August of 1995, nearly five years after Brian's death, I stood in a hospital delivery room trembling with absolute tears of joy running down my face, as my newborn daughter, through adoption, was placed into my awaiting arms. It was such an amazing moment of transformation because after Brian was killed I truly believed I would never experience joy again. Here I was though, reveling in the awesome miracle of this child's birth and the renewal of life she was giving to my wounded family. I knew I had healed 'just enough' the moment I held her and my heart opened up to a flood of joy. Of course, a few weeks later, though blissfully caring for her, I had a rough patch of mother's guilt for feeling joy as if it somehow diminished my love for my son. In my heart, I know nothing ever can, but sometimes I have to quiet my head in order to truly hear the sounds of my heart.

As I write this, I am nearing from the 24th anniversary of my son's death. While easier than the first ones, no anniversary is ever easy. My pain has softened, though. It is softer in that I now remember my son also lived and embrace precious memories of our lives together, more than I focus on how he died. I continue to work with and for crime victims, serving also on our National POMC Board and other crime victim organizations trying to make a difference. I remind myself daily there are more good people in this world than bad, and I have been so fortunate to see and know so many of those people. I learned to have a higher set of priorities since my son's death, don't sweat the small stuff, and truly appreciate what is most important in life. I enjoy the simple things such as a beautiful sunset and value the more profoundly important such as furiously loving my family and friends today, as none of us are guaranteed tomorrow.

Today, I can say I live my life as fully as possible and intend to do so until I no longer have life in me. There was a time I thought I could not continue living. I realize I have survived what I once thought was not survivable and I have turned tragedy into something positive. I did so in memory of my beautiful son whose voice was silenced way too soon. In surviving, I was allowed to continue singing his song, as well as my own, and that of those who have endured what life should never be about.

THE WORST THING
By Carolyn T. Johnson

the worst thing
you can do to a hateful person
be it man or woman who made
your past life miserable
is
when they reach
out for absolution
years later
ignore their emails
leave friend requests unaccepted
neglect to link-in

make them
insignificant

ONE MORE TIME
By Sharon Fulham

    It had been two months since Lou Gehrig's disease claimed the life of my dear friend and I was still distraught. Today, I would get out of my recliner and celebrate the moments we shared instead of feeling depressed. I welcomed the warm sun light as I drove down the freeway toward a favorite coffee shop. I thought about the times I cracked jokes and shared funny stories with her. Giggling she would blurt out, "I hear you!" God, how I wish I could hear those words one more time. When I entered the glass doors of the coffee shop I felt better. She seemed close. It seemed like old times as I placed my order. "May I have a large iced mocha?" I asked. "Oh, and don't forget to pile on the whipped cream!" Giggling, the barista replied, "I hear you!" My heart fluttered with joy as I sat down near a window. "Thank you Lord" I whispered.

A TOUCH OF RED
By Constance Gilbert

As I watch out my front window, a head count is impossible. I see twenty or more sparrows and robins flitting from swaying branch to branch. The leafless tree provides little protection from the rain. They must be resting before continuing their journey.

On this dreary day in January, the robins' red breasts add a bit of color and trigger several memories and thoughts.

Having lived most of my life in southwestern Michigan, robins were the first signs of spring. They are more accurate than Punxsutawney Phil. Here in Central Oregon, the robins stick around. One look at the snow covered Cascade Mountains and I know spring will not be coming in the near future. I feel a bit of disappointment.

As a few more robins came into view, I remember one of the legends about this bird.

The night was so cold and chilly that Mary was unable to keep her newborn infant, Jesus, warm. The wind blew constantly into the drafty stable nearly putting the fire out. Mary was worried and asked the animals for help. But they were asleep along with tired Joseph. Mary nearly lost hope, but then she heard the flapping of a bird's wings. The bird was none other than the brown robin. Seeing Mary's helplessness, he decided to help her keep the stable warm. So, he flapped his wings rigorously at the dying embers, and then fetched some dry sticks. This stopped the fire from going out but a flame that rose suddenly burnt the little bird's breast turning it red. Despite getting hurt, the bird continued his efforts to keep the fire going. Mary was so moved by the kind gesture of this little bird that she blessed the bird in the morning, saying that "From now on, let your red breast be a reminder of your good deed."

As I write this, the scene outside of my window has changed. The wind and rain have disappeared and the sun is shining as it pushes away the clouds. The proud-looking robins are preening their feathers as they rest on the black, skeleton-like tree branches.

Again my thoughts wonder and prayer comes to mind.

When life is stormy, our prayers tend to flit restlessly with the hope that they'll reach God's listening ears. Yet we are not still long enough to hear or see His answer. We just say a quick "Amen" and fly to another branch. We miss the moment when we fell, but were lifted up and returned to a safe branch.

Then I hear God whisper, *Remember Isabel.*

I do, Lord. I handled the hurricane okay, including the power outage, until darkness fell. The wind was fierce as it rattled my windows. The rain beat down in sheets and sounded like hundreds of drumsticks playing a rapid, staccato rhythm on the roof. But it was the tree that scared me.

That huge 100+ year old tree had been leaning toward the house all day and evening creaking and groaning. I was okay as long as I could see it, but now the groaning was like a deep moaning. If it fell, would I be safe? If not, where would I live? Could I save my precious things from blowing away or becoming soaked with polluted rain? Was the decision to stay home alone wise?

What calmed those fears?

You did, Lord.

Remember how... you called out to me.

Yes, I needed to sense your presence. I desired to feel your hand holding mine. I wanted to hear your voice reassuring me. My emotions had overridden my brain. I knew you were in control and could calm the storm or me, but logic wasn't ruling.

I needed "normal" so I phoned my son.

"Mom, are you okay?! We've tried calling and couldn't get through. We've been praying as we watch the weather reports."

I told him I was okay just scared and feeling out of control.

"But what can we do? We're three thousand miles away!"

"Just talk to me... about anything. I need to hear your voice." Even the baby's crying in the background was comforting. An hour later, I hung up, feeling at peace. It seemed quieter outside, too. I turned on the radio. Hurricane Isabel had been downgraded to a tropical storm as it passed us in Richmond, Virginia.

Yes, my child, your son was the voice you needed to hear. He distracted you while I gave you peace. Do you remember that the phone was dead the next time you picked it up? Lines were down everywhere, yet your call went through. As the storm quieted, you slept.

Yes, on the sofa- not in bed, where the tree might have fallen. I remember that my things no longer mattered, because I realized that my work on earth wasn't finished yet. Was it?

You are beginning to understand.

Rest in me. Be still. Listen for my voice. Sing like the birds in praise and thanks. That is their message.

I stop typing and look out my window once more. It's raining again, but there are no red breasts in the tree. Like Mary, I take a moment to silently thank them for their kind deed of flaming my thoughts and memories.

I have been blessed. Now, it is time to sing!

It still is one of my favorite hymns. Knowing He remains in control, I remain content.

HARD LESSON
By Anjali Pursai

Mom brought her home
One early spring evening.
A small black cat, ribs
Showing, tail long,
And one white spot
On her bony chest.
Ragged she looked, but
She purred on our laps
And stole our hearts:
Lucy, the family cat.

Six years old, I could
Not imagine our lives
Without her; but she
Never grew, got thinner,
Ever thinner, wasted
Away until that morning
Mom told my sister and me
To say *Goodbye* before
We left for school.
I never saw her again.

Darkness swooped in,
My pillow wet with tears
Each night; but I tried
To put on a brave face
For my little sister and
Ached inside for Lucy.
Mom knew my pain;
Before long, another black
Cat without a white spot
Came to live with us.

I called her Pepper,
And she became my cat,
Resembled Lucy enough
But not the same: today,
Both hold places in my heart.

ROCK ME
By Jean Varda

Rock me hold me
take me into
your warm silken
embrace
hide me from the
suffering of myself
in the pleasure of you

Rock me hold me
tell me everything is alright
tell me I am safe forever
in your love

Rock me hold me
kiss me lightly
touch me warmly
let me lie in your arms
in the warmth
of your love

THE GATES WERE OPENED
By Anne Hill, Ph.D.

Uncle Alex needed my caresses, but, more importantly, he needed someone to listen to his pain and bolster his fragile ego. By age seven, I was not only in his arms, but helping him cope with everyday problems like time management. Since it was the 1950s and child sexual abuse was still in the closet, whenever I spoke up, I was quickly silenced.

Hence I was continually thrust into the role of Uncle Alex's substitute wife, in almost every sense of the word. As a teen, I rebelled by not going to church and going to the refrigerator instead. Food helped squelch my anger, the sexual feelings Uncle Alex aroused in me and other emotions unacceptable for Catholic girls.

After college, I was 100 pounds overweight and so desperate to get away from Uncle Alex that I eloped with someone who promised to love me forever. But from the wedding night on, my husband, Jason, became increasingly abusive in every way. Unbeknownst to me, Jason was a psychopath who engaged in corrupt practices and had criminal connections.

Also unbeknownst to me, Jason suffered from paranoia and constantly accused me of plotting to kill him or steal money. As his paranoia progressed, he blamed his deteriorating mental abilities and his failing career on my "rays." He believed that I had rays emanating from various parts of my body that were capable of destroying his mental and physical powers. At times he imagined snipers and witches and thought I was poisoning or blinding him.

Some of Jason's abuse stemmed from his sadism, but some, from his need to protect himself from my rays. Hence, in addition to the social isolation, extreme verbal abuse, rape, and hitting typical of abusers, Jason frequently confined me in various rooms lest my rays enfeeble him. Towards the end I was locked in the attic, then the basement; rarely allowed to see our children; and subject to lengthy Nazi-style interrogations during which Jason tried to uncover my secret plots against him. He also researched and then imitated other forms of Nazi psychological torture and terrorized me into submission by scalding one child, drugging and scarring the other, and hitting both of them.

I tried to leave Jason, but he threatened to maim or kill me or the children. Since Jason knew hit men and I'd seen him hurt the children, I couldn't take the chance that he might carry through on these threats.

The police failed to respond to my calls. Even the pediatrician was no help. At the time, laws against domestic violence were not only weak, but rarely enforced. There were no battered women's shelters and Jason had all the money. Despite my full-time job as a psychologist at a clinic, Jason had taken control of my paycheck and all our assets.

I had no checkbook or credit card and, to complete my confinement at home, Jason installed special locks on all the doors so I couldn't escape. And by threatening to kill my boss if my boss didn't keep tabs on me and report to him daily about my activities, Jason was able to monitor me at work too. (My boss was too terrified of Jason and Jason's criminal connections to call the police.)

After nine years of entrapment, however, the gate was miraculously opened and the children and I escaped. We had no money and no place to go, but help was provided.

For the next four years I battled Jason for custody of the children. All totaled, there were fifty-four court or court-related appearances, including five separate mental health investigations, one of which lasted nine months.

Back then joint custody was non-existent. But Jason persuaded the judge to have us evaluated by a social worker who proved to be the judge's lover. She was also a friend and associate of Jason's lawyer. By twisting around psychological terms, she convinced the court to coerce me into a shared custody arrangement that scarred the children for decades.

Furthermore, since no-fault divorce had yet to be instituted and Jason had doctored our financial records, he was awarded nine-tenths of our assets.

But one night when Jason had locked me in the basement and wanted to burn me alive, I found God. God and the many people he sent my way gave me the strength to endure, and my children became honest non-abusive parents and dedicated helping professionals. They have scars, but the cycle of abuse has been broken.

I'm scarred too, but, thanks to Uncle Alex and Jason, I learned to carefully listen to people and be sensitive to their emotions and needs. This has helped me in my relationships and my work as a therapist. Jason also taught me about the inner workings of the paranoid mind, which I've been able to use to help paranoid individuals and their families.

I also gained compassion for human suffering as a result of domestic terrorism. Even today, many people don't understand why an abused person can't just walk away or how an abuser can gain control over a person by preying on that person's vulnerabilities, manipulating them with guilt, isolating them, putting them in double binds, forcing them to betray their values, and threatening their loved ones — methods as powerful as physical force.

Even today, some psychologists talk about abuse victims being "codependent" or "addicted to drama." But I understand how people can become trapped and then hate themselves for being trapped. So when victims share their stories, I can validate the invisible chains which bind them. In some cases, the fact that someone believed them and didn't blame them for their own pain made the difference between life and death. And when individuals, frustrated by years of delays and mistreatment by the courts or some other institution, talk about committing murder or suicide, I understand how they've come to that point and have been able to talk them out of it.

In my forty some years as a psychologist, I've been blessed with opportunities to use my experiences with domestic abuse, sexual assault and injustice to help many hundreds of people directly as a therapist and, through my numerous articles and presentations, hundreds of thousands more. I say this not to boast of myself, but in gratitude for having been able to use whatever I suffered to help others.

For example, during my court years I became too depressed to be able to do therapy, and was subsequently demoted to clerical work at a make-shift "testing center" designed by my supervisor so I wouldn't be fired. As I grew stronger, however, I helped transform this into a center that helped people find work and improve their communication skills.

The gates were also opened for me to establish programs specially designed for victims of abuse, job harassment and other forms of mistreatment. And it was with great pleasure that I conducted psychological evaluations for persons involved in legal battles who were struggling to counter the damaging effects of prior mental health evaluations written by hardhearted, self-serving mental health professionals like the judge's lover.

Because of her, and several corrupt court officials, I was aware of all the tricky clever ways that psychological terms and theories could be used to destroy people and deprive them of their rights. Hence I was able to write powerful rebuttals to alleged psychological evaluations that were shams and insults to the profession. Fueled by my anger and pain, I was motivated to read any book and research study I could find that would help these people.

Many times it was my report that prevented innocent people from being crucified in the courts by reports full of lies and misinformation. I give all the credit to God because without God, I wouldn't have survived.

My experiences also taught me that healing takes time. Hence I can encourage survivors who are frustrated with the recovery process. After all, it's taken me the last half of my life to "get over" the first half. I've also learned that "moving forward" doesn't mean forgetting about the past, but taking it with me and using it for good.

I still grieve and hurt sometimes, but that's okay because I've also learned that I don't need to be happy all the time in order to love, be loved and live to good purpose.

GLIMMER OF HOPE
By Lynn C. Johnston

Shattered lives and shattered hearts
Shattered worlds torn apart
Tattered clothes and tattered dreams
Life blown asunder, so it seems

From the dark of night, all is lost
Devastation too high to count the cost
Yet amidst all the misery that abounds
A glimmer of hope can somehow be found

In an open heart and an outstretched hand
A compassionate smile helps us understand
We're not alone in our desperate plight
Someone can help us win our fight

With a little faith and a little hope
We'll find some peace and a way to cope
Thanks in part to someone who cared
Who was willing to give and willing to share

PILGRIMAGE
By Judith Lyn Sutton

Joy on North Kaanapali Beach
Where each summer I journey,
Each morning watch the sun
Slip over West Maui Mountains

As he unfurls his great shining
Across the slate-blue channel
Graced by a mystic placement
Of islands, awaiting his touch.

Sitting on the lanai with pen
Sliding over paper, I chronicle
Dawn's daily miracle, rejoice
Over light subduing darkness

When rays first manifested,
Lit the world ages ago just so
Flora and fauna could thrive.
Still, redbirds revel in the glow

As dolphins leap, spin, and dive.
From the deep, a pair of turtles
Glide on the coral reef, bask
Warm, alone before they mate.

All around me, Maui awakens
As the singular blue of waves
Becomes a palette: pale green
To sapphire at the horizon; and

Palms tango with trade-winds.
Each July and August, I lose
Myself in this song of spirit--
Of trees, turtles, billows, birds.

Their harmony first healed me
From cancer, taught me to reach
For lenity of life, returned me
Home yearly revived, restored.

AWAKENING
By Rosemary McKinley

I never really understood what losing a loved one meant because I had never experienced this wrenching event. When other people lost a parent or grandparent, I would say some comforting words that I thought would help but I didn't really feel the pain.

Then, in 2001, it happened to me. My mother, whom I had been close to all my life, died. She had a chronic type of leukemia for about seven years. She went through much agony and pain near the end. We children felt so helpless watching her suffer so. It was so sad. She soldiered though three bouts of chemo for a month at a time over a year and a half. Dad, my brother, and I were there by her side every time. We prayed for her while we supported her and tried to give much encouragement. The nurses at the Don Monti Cancer Center were wonderful with their cheery personalities and funny stories about their children and parents. Mom's doctor also was so understanding and encouraging. She always had another round of medications or suggestions when a problem arose in her treatment.

The discouraging elements of this ordeal were what wasn't said. Mom would meet people she knew in the community at the Center when she went for an appointment. Over the months, she and Dad would learn that they passed away. Their treatment only worked for so long. Dad would tell me who had died but didn't announce it to Mom. Little by little, there were fewer faces that they recognized.

When the time came for Mom to choose hospice, she made the decision with our support, again. It was a very gloomy time. My brothers, Dad, and I were at her side as much as we could be every day until the end. The last night of her life, my brother called me back, as I had just left. He knew I wanted to be there with her. I had never seen someone die before and especially not someone I loved dearly. It is an event I will not forget. After, I was mostly in a daze and miserable when I wasn't crying. I made it through the planning of the arrangements because I had my family there. I just couldn't think of anything else but Mom. It was as if a movie was playing in my head of different childhood events when I was a little girl. Mom took me strawberry picking or I would be at one of my brother's birthday parties or at day trips to the beach. These memories were comforting, visual, and visceral. She was still with me, I felt.

I was in my early fifties at the time and had planned on teaching until my sixties. Everything changed on the day she died and moved forward. My grief turned into determination.

When all of the services were over and I went back to school, I kept thinking, "How much time do I have left?" What do I really want to do with the rest of my life? Slowly but surely I came to a decision. I wanted to make a career change. I still liked teaching but I had been a teacher for close to thirty years. I wanted to do something different; I wanted to become a writer.

Interestingly, I had attended Columbia Teachers' College Writing Institute in the early '90's to become a better writing teacher. It was a wonderful experience in many ways. I had to learn how to teach writing workshop which immersed children in writing by having them pen something important to them every day. From those entries, the student had to look for a thread or theme and write a piece on it after a month or so. It helped the students focus on what they were interested in and this led to better writing. It worked for me the first time I had to go through the process so I could see how it worked first hand. However, through this experience I had never once thought about becoming an author. The story I wrote during that first try was about something that had happened to me as a teacher. That thread came through by reading my notebook over and over, loud and clear. I did notice that others in my class seemed to want to write for publication. They didn't say that but it seemed evident to me.

All these years later I was bitten by the writing bug. So in 2003, I retired so that I could write full time. Funny thing is that I didn't know anything about this new career and I was leaving one that I had mastered. I was a novice but I was willing to learn even though I had no idea how difficult it was to become a published author.

Every morning I would take a cup of coffee up to my home office and write about my childhood. I called them "glimpses" because these were short pieces. All the time I was thinking of Mom and how important she was featured in these stories. Then I found some places to submit my writing in Poets &Writers. I began sending stories by snail mail because I didn't know how to send an attachment. I then had to write a cover letter each time. That was more of a pain that sending my work. I finally asked for help and learned how to send an attachment. My writing life became so much easier.

As many authors will tell you, rejections come in leaps and bounds especially in the beginning of a career. All of my work ended up being rejected! It was quite discouraging, even though I had read in several free writers' newsletters that this is to be expected. Yet, I persevered. I signed up for a few writing courses at a local college and kept writing every day. I found a writers' group and joined, as well. It gave me a reason to keep going because I had to have something polished to share with the group. It forced me to keep on writing.

Then one day I saw in a local paper that there was an essay contest sponsored by the Visiting Nurse Association of Oyster Bay. That was the same agency that had sent the best nurses to care for my mother after one of her hospital stays. The topic was: The Joys of Growing Older. Basically I wrote that after reevaluating my life, I became a writer and spent time doing what I wanted, like going to Broadway plays with my friends and caring for my Dad. My essay came in third place and earned a monetary prize. It was thrilling.

After that essay contest win, another story that was accepted was about my mother the night she died. I was happy that one of my first successful stories was about her; the reason I became a writer. She would have been happy for me, too.

That was the beginning of more acceptances and a request to write a nonfiction local history book that I gladly accepted. All of these successes were layered with rejections and a determination to succeed.

What I had not bargained for was the challenge of this new career and what it did for me. Now I can call it a career but there were years in the beginning that I wondered if I had done the right thing by retiring. Yet focusing in on writing, researching and honing my word skills was all consuming. Surprisingly, this challenge was just what I needed to keep me on a positive path. Working toward a difficult goal kept me on track after Mom died and has eventually become fulfilling. She would have liked that.

HEARTHSTONE
By Karissa Dong

Within the bleak confines
Of these walls, I could not care
For the world outside—
No sweet scent of winter
Enticed my inner hearth,
For even the wind's breath
Proved always too cold
To stoke my withering flame.
So indoors, I hid away
Until I could no longer recall
How lively the fire's dance
Felt upon my hearthstone.
And yet, within me,
Ever a quiet longing
For the lost voice I loved,
And the dear caress I knew;
For now, I heard only
The gales lament and now,
I felt only the leaves quiver—
And I ached for reprieve.
So donning scarf and jacket,
I sought backcountry roads
And took a climb to the crest,
Where I breathed
The crispness of pines,
Watched the blue world
Swirl its celestial fingers
In a vast, rippling lake
Like the dainty play of a child.
Only then, lost in nature's reverie,
Did my heart's disquiet depart—
For but a moment long
Enough for my fire to flicker,
Stir anew upon the hearth.

NOTHING LASTS FOREVER, BUT...
By Wendy Wolf

When I was young,
we always had dogs.
A succession of them.
My mother was fearful;
a dog meant security.
Big dogs with deep voices
and gentle souls.
In the beginning, I loved them all.
But my mother had no tolerance for an animal's mistakes--
a soiled carpet, a shoe destroyed,
and the dog was gone,
driven away and dumped in a field.
"Someone nice will find them," she'd say.

One of those dogs was my best friend.
A German Shepherd;
I named her Thorne,
for a comic book heroine I admired.
She followed me everywhere;
my companion, my guard.
At night, I snuggled in her soft fur.
I taught her things; she was calm and smart.
I still have the red and blue ribbons we won.

One day, she chewed the side
of an ugly, gold sofa.
It wasn't a big hole, but big enough.
I came home from school and she was gone.
I didn't cry;
we were punished for crying.
Instead, I held the hurt inside,
and I made a vow never to become attached again.
Soon there was another dog.

(A Husky with blue eyes? I'm not sure.)
I knew he wouldn't be there long.

A few dogs later, my mother pursed her lips and said,
"I never should have gotten rid of Thorne.
She was the best dog we ever had."
She said it casually,
as if reconsidering the color of paint on the walls.
I sat there unable to breathe,
bound and wounded by the thought
that taking away someone I loved so much
had happened on nothing more than a whim.
And she did it over and over again.

Years later, my husband observed
my "barriers" to love
(remnants of my vow),
but once past the hurdle, I was all in.
It didn't take long.

We adopted two tiny, striped kittens.
Merlin, troublesome, orange, and full of light,
and Morgaine, grey-black, brave and full of heart.
Thirteen years later, Morgaine's kidneys failed.
We had six months together after that.
A terrible time, and a fragile gift.

In the end, I held her still, warm body,
and even in the midst of grief,
there was one bittersweet consolation
(and I was thankful) …

That for the first time,
I had a lifetime
with someone I loved.

THE OTHER SIDE OF THE STARS
By Lola Di Giulio De Maci

"I'm sorry. It's cancer." The voice on the other end of the line was steady and direct. A voice that had undoubtedly said these same words many times before. But this was the first time those words were directed at me. My blood ran cold.

"Cancer," I repeated, swallowing hard like there was a huge lump in my throat. "No woman wants to hear that she has breast cancer," I heard my voice say.

"And I don't want to leave my children," I pleaded. My words filled the gray silence of the room.

I hung up the phone, stunned and frightened. Now what? Where do I go from here? How do I tell my children? It was the eve of my fifty-fifth birthday.

The afternoon sun quietly melted into the evening shadows, as I waited for my children to come home. I was grateful they were close by – my daughter teaching school a few miles away and my son attending a nearby university. In a somewhat-rational corner of my mind, I tried rehearsing how I would tell them about the call I received earlier that day. I prayed God would help me find the right words.

I was in the midst of preparing dinner when my daughter came home. She placed her books on the table and leaned up against the kitchen counter, as she had done dozens of times before. I looked at my child like I was seeing her for the very first time. It took all the courage I had to tell my daughter that her mother had breast cancer.

"I'm going to make it," I promised, holding her tightly in my arms. "I'm going to be okay."

We stood there, holding each other, for what seemed like an eternity. My daughter. My child. I didn't want to let her go. Not now. Not ever.

Later that evening, I sat my son and daughter down on the couch in the living room and told them what the doctor had said. I assured them that everything was going to be all right. I would never leave them. Ever. I couldn't.

I'll never forget the looks on their faces. Confusion. Fear. Concern. Their expressions are etched in my soul forever.

As I sat looking at my two beautiful children sitting there before me, I couldn't help but think of my third and last child, a baby daughter, who had left me shortly after birth to live on the other side of the stars. I pictured her sitting alongside her brother and sister, listening to every word I was saying. I wanted her here with me tonight. I needed all three of my children. I couldn't face tomorrow without them.

My son was the first to say good-night. It was a little after 10 p.m. I gently embraced him. "I'm going to be all right," I whispered, recognizing that familiar lump in my throat.

As he headed down the hallway toward his bedroom, the ground began to rumble. The glass objects on the coffee table and in the china closet vibrated and rattled, while the floor beneath our feet seemed to move in waves across the room. Our house shook from top to bottom. We had just experienced an earthquake centered twelve miles north of our city. It took place at 10:08 p.m.

What are the chances of having an earthquake right then? I asked myself. And centered so close to home. I was convinced that the heavens had opened just for me. I felt as if my baby daughter, my third child, was here with me, too. A beautiful peace filled my soul. A quiet joy. Hope.

Twenty years of afternoon suns have quietly melted into the evening shadows since the day I received that phone call from the surgeon. I take each brand-new day and live it as best I can, chasing all the dreams I still have left to dream.

And my children...I have lived to see my son become a psychologist and my daughter continue down her path as a teacher. To know that they are living their dreams warms my heart.

And even though my world was rocked from top to bottom by two forces I had no control over – a cancer and an earthquake – I don't doubt for a moment that someone was watching over me from the other side of the stars.

Somehow I knew I would make it.

And I did.

FINDING MY RELIGION
By Sheree K. Nielsen

Two days passed since my coworker Jack reported for work. Always prompt and considerate, it was unlike him not to call. Most mornings Jack's entrance into the break room was far from boring. Singing the lyrics from an alternative rock song, he poured himself a cup of coffee chanting "that's me in the corner, that's me in the spotlight, losing my religion, trying to keep up with you. And I don't know if I can do it..." Pretty soon everyone in the area was laughing, joining in on the chorus.

By the third day, his boss, Willie, feeling unsettled regarding Jack's whereabouts, placed a phone call to the police. An hour later, Willie met the officers at Jack's apartment door. A knock yielded no response, and the police entered the residence.

They found Jack, dead, propped up in a chair with a cloth over his head. A gun lay nearby and dried blood spattered the wall behind him. That was Jack - so polite as not to make a big mess. Always thinking ahead, he left behind a suicide note and a living will.

Days prior to his suicide, Jack complimented his department manager, Kevin, on his beautiful family and loving wife. Oh, how Jack yearned to find his true love.

Every time that song played on the radio; I couldn't help but be reminded of Jack. Why would such an incredibly smart man wish to end his life? Was his search for the perfect woman too much to bear? Did he live by words of the song?

I hoped I would never reach a low point similar to Jack's in my life.

By the winter of 1994, I'd hit rock bottom. In financial distress, lied to and cheated on, I reached my breaking point with my husband. After twelve years of marriage, divorce papers were filed. As a gift to myself, I joined a yoga class to deal with stress.

To ward off loneliness, three girlfriends filled my schedule with shopping, drinking, and parties. 'Morning after' results gave way to dark circles under my eyes and migraine headaches. My calendar already full, I started dating. The New Year brought lazy, negative, and egotistical men my way. I reflected on the song lyrics "every whisper of every waking hour I'm choosing my confessions." Fatigued from a week's worth of activities, I spent Sunday mornings reading the newspaper in bed.

Feeling like something had to give, I took a break from men and partying. I hung out with friends, watched movies, played board games and listened to mellow music. Dating was replaced with praying. Unsure how to pray correctly, I let it all spill out. Whatever came to mind, that's what God heard. I prayed a lot.

A year after my divorce, I asked one of my best friends, Russell, on a date. Three years later, I married him. Friends and family gathered at our May Day celebration as we exchanged vows on the picturesque grounds of a white stone mansion at sunset.

I thought about my life's path and purpose. The importance of finding a church with a 'common thread' where hubby and I could flourish weighed on my mind.

My longtime friend Tina grew disenchanted with her place of worship and spoke of a new church. During a phone conversation late one Saturday night, she invited me to a non-denominational service the following morning. "Don't let all the singing scare you," she warned.

On Sunday morning I met Tina inside the church entryway. Heart stammering, I took a deep breath and followed her to a pew.

Unaccustomed to a service this joyous, I felt jubilant as the congregation's melodic voices rang throughout the church.

As I heard the words to "I Surrender All", tears streamed down my cheeks. My body trembled, overcome with emotion. Hard as I tried, I couldn't stop the flood waters. Nor did I want to. Through the next song, and the next, I sobbed as the Holy Spirit filled me up, cleansing my soul, helping me find my religion.

The pastor's sermon keyed in on making a difference in others' lives and finding one's divine purpose. I listened intently. After the sermon, he uncovered a huge board propped on an easel. The board revealed hundreds of red-looped ribbons.

Pastor Tim requested each church member and visitor to step forward and remove three ribbons and pins from the board.

"Think of three people in your life that have made a difference, and pin them."

I pinned Tina, my longtime friend, who comforted me through the lean years of my first marriage, forever listening, never judging, and providing a safe haven when I needed a good cry. Hundreds of people, all around, were hugging and pinning. And hugging.

I placed the other two ribbons in my coat pocket.

Once home, I found my husband reading a book in the bedroom. I pinned a red ribbon on his bright white t-shirt and kissed his cheek.

Surprised he asked, "What's this for?"
"For making a difference in my life."
"Good service?"
"The best."

The following Sunday, I arose, ate a light breakfast of raspberries and oatmeal, dressed in my Sunday best, and grabbed the keys to the car. Already two steps ahead, Russell met me in the garage wearing nice slacks and a sweater.

After church service, we drove to Spencer Manor, a nursing home, where my elderly mother resided. There I pinned the final red ribbon on the once strong, now frail woman that brought me into this world as I thanked her for the gift of life. Confined to a wheelchair, she smiled, but said nothing. Due to her dementia, Mom probably didn't comprehend much of what was spoken, but watching her shine was proof enough for me.

Although I had lost my religion over a decade ago, as the popular song lyrics stated, somewhere in between Jack and three beautiful red ribbons, I found it again.

ALONG FOR THE RIDE
By Ann Reisfeld Boutte

It was a cloudless day in April, temperature in the mid-seventies, as I stood behind barricades at the finish line of the MS 150, a two-day bicycle ride from Houston to Austin. My husband, André, was one of thousands of riders on the 150-plus-mile course, an annual fundraiser for the Multiple Sclerosis Society. Andre was a first time rider. He was also an MS patient.

The journey began one evening when André returned home from work and announced he had made an appointment with our family doctor. He had developed some troubling symptoms – a numbness in his left arm and some difficulty speaking. I sat motionless as an electric current shot through my system.

The next week, I accompanied him to his appointment. The doctor performed a series of tests using needles to prick André's arms and legs. When he finished, he referred him to a neurologist. Two weeks later, the neurologist repeated the tests, added a few others, and scheduled an MRI.

André told me to sit down when he telephoned from his office with the MRI results. He had just spoken with the neurologist who said the test had shown a lesion in his brain that could be a tumor. Because of its location, biopsy or surgery would be impossible. The doctor recommended that André wait six weeks and have a second MRI to determine if the lesion had grown and if radiation therapy should be started.

André remained calm, perhaps to reassure me. But as soon as we hung up, I phoned the doctor myself. I was desperate for some words of comfort, which he provided by telling me it was far too soon to make a diagnosis.

As the weeks went by, we were relieved to find that André's symptoms were subsiding, a situation, we reasoned, that would be precluded by a growing tumor. That was confirmed by the second MRI, which showed that the initial lesion was smaller, but that others had developed. The doctor said that André might be suffering a series of small strokes and referred him to a specialist in the Texas Medical Center.

André, who hadn't missed a day of work, was drawing on reserves of strength. But I felt like I was crumbling. I found myriad reasons to phone his office. If he failed to answer, I continued calling at brief intervals until I reached him. Meanwhile, I pictured him unconscious on his office floor.

Once, when he was twenty minutes late for our lunch date, I began pacing back and forth in front of the restaurant, oblivious to a soft drizzle. By the time he arrived and explained that he had forgotten the directions and gotten lost, I was tearfully selecting pallbearers for his funeral.

Nights were more difficult. I spent many early morning hours lying sleepless in terror, trying to recall prayers from Scriptures I had memorized during my confirmation year at age thirteen.

The stroke specialist scheduled another battery of tests over a three-day hospital stay and promised a diagnosis shortly after their completion. The prospect of an answer was a relief. A cerebral arteriogram revealed that André's arteries were clear and eliminated the possibility of strokes. The doctor suggested that a spinal tap would prove definitive, and he was right.

In consultation with a doctor who treats MS patients, we were told that the disease affects each patient differently, crippling some and only minimally impacting others. He noted that André's symptoms were mild, advised him to go on with life as usual, and return if his symptoms worsened. André had to come to terms with the knowledge that he has an incurable, progressive disease. But I rejoiced that he has something he can live with.

Sometime later, he arrived home with another announcement. He said the exhaustive battery of tests he had undergone had confirmed that, except for MS, he was essentially healthy. He said he was grateful for the gift and was determined not to take it for granted. With that in mind, he had signed up to ride with his company team in the MS 150.

I praised his outlook and ambition and encouraged his participation. Secretly, I doubted that he could do it. He was sixty, out of shape, and a bit overweight. A once-a-week tennis game was the extent of his exercise routine. He knew nothing about cycling and didn't even own a bicycle.

On a cold February morning, André joined the team for his first training ride with a bike borrowed from a neighbor. As he pedaled off, shouts called him back. He was handed a helmet and told it was against the rules to ride without one. Jack, the team captain, assessed the situation and decided to ride with the rookie. If he had not, André's cycling career would have ended the day it began.

When they stopped to rest after seven miles, André was winded and spent. His legs were so rubbery that when he got off the bike, he collapsed. But Jack just laughed, called him quite the acrobat, and offered encouragement.

By the end of the day, he had ridden twenty-eight miles and was more determined than ever. Two days later, he bought a twenty-one-speed road bike, a helmet, and Spandex cycling togs.

In his third week of training, André covered forty-two miles. By mid-March, he completed a sixty-mile course, all against a head wind. Between weekend rides, he attended cycling classes at a nearby gym. By the week before the April MS 150 event, André had logged more than nine hundred training miles through all kinds of weather and road conditions and felt strong and confident, if a little apprehensive.

Before dawn, I drove André to the starting point for the first leg of the ride. He joined his teammates for coffee and doughnuts as they checked their gear, aired their tires, and applied liberal coatings of sun block. An atmosphere of fortitude and camaraderie pervaded the gathering.

At six o'clock, I wished him good luck, kissed him goodbye, and went home to make my own preparations to meet him one hundred miles away at the overnight stopping point in La Grange. On the drive, I listened to Country-and-Western music and marveled that anyone could travel the distance on less than four wheels.

Waiting with the crowd in La Grange, I struck up a conversation with the woman next to me who sat in a chair, a cane nearby. She said she had MS and was there to cheer the riders. I told her of my situation.

Hours went by with no sign of André. As the trail of riders thinned, I began to worry. The woman suggested that my husband had sagged in, or climbed aboard one of the support vans that canvas the route for riders in trouble who have to stop. I made my way through the maze of team tents to André's company tent and asked another rider if she knew of his whereabouts. Recognizing my anxiety, she smiled and assured me he was fine, just riding at his own pace.

At seven p.m., André rolled in, smiling. Although his late arrival meant he'd missed dinner, he was happy to shower at a nearby school gymnasium and get to his cot before nine o'clock lights out. Again, I wished him good luck and left for Austin where, with some degree of guilt, I climbed into a comfortable bed in a carpeted and air-conditioned hotel room.

I rose early the next day, eager to get to the finish line to watch the riders and wait for André. As I stood there amid the fans cheering and applauding as clusters of cyclists in brightly colored Spandex rolled by, I knew that long stretches of back roads and highways, stiff head winds, and ribbons of muscle-burning hills were just a few of the obstacles to overcome.

WALKING
By Theresa M. Leslie

Crackling gravel, crunching leaves,
My footsteps punctuate the silence,
Reminding me I will never walk
Again with you, feel you beside me
Hand in hand, in a heart to heart,
Mother and daughter. No more will
I hear your voice as we hike trails
Among the redwoods, up the hills,
Or by the streams in dappled sun.
And yet, as I pause for a moment,
I realize you are here all around me.

HEALING FROM TRAUMA
By Judy Shepps Battle

Crashing to hell's surface
fear/panic/nausea rise
so young, so small
so wanting to run away
so needing to stay.

Help me!

I hear you my youngest self
your shock and hurt
terror and paralysis
buried rage as you
relive imprinted traumas

I am here to help you!

We have wings now
to fly beyond the past
Strong feet
to walk away from any abuse

A mighty voice to shout
No! (without explaining)
No! (without staying)
No! (without apology)

We don't have to remain
in unending pain

Or explain
why we are not guilty

Or understand
the whys, lies, sighs, or byes
of family perpetrators

Or drink/drug/shrug the memory of
double-meaning hugs

My dearest Little Jude
Our healing lies in not becoming them

Not begging one last time for recognition
Not scampering for scattered crumbs

Our healing is a sober surrender to the Infinite
a love story between all parts of self
a sharing with those of like spirit

a celebration of radiant freedom
danced freely in April's warm sunshine.

THE NURSE
By Helen Carson

She was a nurse and proud of it!
Her license said so.
A cancer nurse indeed.
Young and sweet
Swishy white uniform, squeaky shoes
With lofty goals

Making a difference.
Saving lives
Drying tears,
Hugging the pain.
So she thought,
Until that day

They told her she had it too.
Breast cancer, her doctor said.
She would have to have them both removed
Immediately; the day after her honeymoon!
She cried and railed, and retched with fear
And then she knew

She had never really made a difference.
How could she have?
She had not felt the rage and terror
The sleepless dreams of death and loss
Her future, her life, her legacy
Or been so ill she wished to die,

Until the day the surgeon removed
The bandages and she looked down with tears
At the angry red gash where her breasts had been.
Breasts that had betrayed the woman within,
Subtle maybe, but seductive still,
And then she knew what her patients knew.

No one could make a difference.
No healer, no parent, no spouse, no friend.
The journey was made alone.
It was long…and cold…and dark.
But now when she met their eyes, they knew
She had finally become…the nurse.

SPEAKING THE LANGUAGE OF MOMENTS
By Roshanda Johnson

This man didn't break my heart. He tore it so that the edges were too jagged to ever be properly pieced together again. Here I was giving him "my everything" only to have everything not be enough. He wanted to give his first love "a second try." Who does that? Besides, he was my first love...well...maybe not my FIRST love, but Jamar* was my first attempt at loving consciously and with reason; my first attempt at loving someone as I loved myself. Isn't that sort of a big deal? I had really screwed over a great guy in a previous relationship so I entered "Us" with purpose. I purposed to love so powerfully that I could reverse the direction of karma. I set out to tailor my love to his needs and undo any damage that had been done with the intensity of my love. And it wasn't enough. He left, taking with him the currency of my self-worth, to build a life with his "first love." I was emotionally bankrupt. I had invested so much of myself in him and in turn he embezzled my hopes and dreams. This betrayal was irreparable. I breathed but did not live.

Then he called me one overcast, November day and said, "I miss you. You were my best friend." I fumbled for my journal. I was prepared for this moment and had already written the script for this scene because I KNEW that one day he'd come calling and I'd get my chance to say (flipping through my notebook), "How dare you call me after all this time! You shattered my spirit! I couldn't have loved you better if I was God. I made time come undone and simultaneously stand still for you. I gave you the marrow of my bones, a chance at living when you were found dying." (Dramatic, right?) Needless to say, what actually came out of my mouth was something more like, "I miss you too." Where had that come from? How could my mouth betray my emotions and allow the words "I miss you too" to slip from my subconscious? Did I really miss him? How could I still love a man that had once stripped the life from my veins?

Seconds stretched as silence played pendulum between our phone cords. Fearing what would come out of my mouth, I refused to open it. "I am not asking for a second chance," he finally said. "I just want my friend back." If he wanted his friend back, then he was indeed asking me for something, right?

Was he asking me to turn the other cheek and risk getting slapped on that one as well? Asking me to forget that he left me for history and now wanted "Us" to repeat itself? I couldn't do that...

Fast forward five months later and he's stretched out on my new faux-leather couch snoring as I sit, IPad in hand, typing this...whatever this is... and smiling at that funny thing he did yesterday while we were tasting wedding cakes. Don't let the transition between paragraphs fool ya. This evolution has not been easy. I have my moments of doubt. From time to time, when it's way past the hour I expect him, I slip into a panic. I start in with that familiar What if? mantra that in no way helps my progress towards nirvana, but then I catch myself. I literally open my physical arms to catch my spiritual self and to communicate with my fears. I remind my fears that I do not choose them, I choose love. I choose forgiveness.

I truly never thought I could love again, but I realized that my worst day with Jamar is better than my best day with any other person on the planet. Besides, while brokenness was kicking the crap out of me, I learned a valuable lesson. Humans make mistakes, and for every wrong anyone has ever done to me, I have done as much (or worse) to myself. And if I, in my misguided moments, could wrong myself, it stands to reason that some other person could misstep as well. So when my mind let my mouth say, "I miss you too" what it really meant was, "Jamar, you did not mean to hurt me. You're just as lost in these dimensions of time as any other Alice."

Who knew there'd be a better ME in the ashes? And this new woman is radically committed to redemption and with each moment is capable of extending to Jamar (or anyone) that which we all stand in need of, LOVE. Not that pop culture definition love that we tend to throw around these days, but that "I am willing to see beyond the things you have done to who and what you eternally are" love. I now consciously communicate with love in a way I never knew my once selfish heart could and love only answers to a certain language, the language of moments. Love knows that she has the power to use this moment to shape the perceptions of the last moment while simultaneously shaping the destiny of the next. Her language says, "Hey, that stuff from back then sucked, but this moment has the potential to be sweeeeeetttttt!"

Don't mistake me, the language of moments does not make us forget wholly, but it does burn away the sting and leave the golden lesson shining in its stead. Jamar and I both had lessons to learn through the testing and trials of our relationship. Jamar loved me, but he loved her as well. He would have forever been anchored to the past had he not given his first love the chance to redeem herself. He found out that sometimes your first love isn't your last; that people change because they are supposed to; that his future should not look like his past. Did it hurt him to find out? Yes. Did it hurt me while he was finding out? Yes. But as a result he is a better man in the present. And don't let me forget the strings I pulled in OUR unraveling. I purposed to love him as I love myself and that's exactly what I did. The problem was…he was not and still is not me! He needed me to love him for who he was, even when he was human.

I must admit, we are better after our breakdown. The old building was razed, leaving us an empty, open space to rebuild. (By the way, sometimes void is a good thing…I hear God pulled a universe from it.) Through communication based in love and not fear we have stitched together seams thought rent beyond repair. The language of "this moment" serves as a thread holding us together and offers multiple opportunities to begin again. In and out Jamar and I go through the fabric of time, stitching the frayed portions, making tiny little sutures in the present that are incapable of being pulled apart by the past.

How can one restore to sound condition feelings that have been bruised beyond recognition? What do we do when the injuries are so severe that any sense of oneness we once had is lying under so many layers of scar tissue that it would require further cutting to reveal they ever existed? We repair by communicating love through the language of moments. Too often we cannot move forward because we are diligently working at mastering the word, yesterday. Yesterday is a word and not a language. It is unintelligible to today; unintelligible to our hearts. Our hearts want to move forward. Our hearts want to forgive. Our hearts want us to decide tomorrow can be different; they want us to give them a reason to beat another day. To do this we must not let history override the power of right now. This isn't easy, but it is possible. It takes effort. It requires that we consciously replace negative thoughts that wish to beset us, with words and actions that free us. It means choosing healing, not just waiting on healing to come. It is the post-it note stuck to our minds that reads "Part of being a human being is…BEING!" Admittedly, the language of moments is a difficult language to become skilled in, and I had to be subjugated to a very dark place to acquire it, but I like the woman I am now. I like to think I am using my ashes as mortar to build a temple whose inscription reads: "Now is here. I welcome it. Love is here. I embrace it. Thank you, Time, for handing us this moment because in this moment we realize that we start over again, pick up at the end, find out through our trials that love only begins again."

-- *Names have been changed to protect the innocent:)

RELEASE
By Aarya Mecwan

Try as I may, I cannot fall asleep.
The pink luminescent clock hands read midnight,
And my mind still travels round and round
Like a hamster on a wheel.

The answer never comes to my ceaseless question
What shall I do with my life?
Over and over, it echoes inside my head

I throw the covers off the bed,
Get up and dressed, wrapping my knitted scarf
Around my neck, putting my stupid-looking
Red and brown beanie on my head.

Grabbing my keys, I open the door
And head downstairs only to find
It's freezing outside and takes my breath away.

I guess for tonight, that's a good thing.
As I head down the abandoned streets,
The overwhelming question repeats
Itself with each step I take

I stumble into a lonely coffee shop at 1 a.m.,
Leave my order, and head back to the streets.
My brown boots follow each other

Out into the nebulous night
Until I stop in front of a sleepy house
Fronted by a low wall where I sit at last,
Leave my head, and look at the stars.

Spellbound by the separateness of each,
I realize they all have found their place
As I, in time, will find mine.

CHILD IN THE PICTURE
By Lynn C. Johnston

Child in the picture
Sweetness radiates from thee
Rapture fills your heart
As you imagine what could be

The world will be your oyster
Thrilling notions fill your head
You nestle in their visions
While dreaming silently in bed

Child in the picture
Did the world do right by you
Was the pleasure worth the pain
That nearly tore your heart in two

Were you protected from the evil
That befell so many hearts
Were you sanctioned from above
To overcome and stand apart

Child in the picture
Can you still dream of what might be
Now that you're no longer
The young girl that once was me

KEEPSAKES
By Jane Blanchard

For months dust fell upon the ring, size ten,
inscribed to you from me. The bedside stand
bore well the weight of love abandoned. When
you came back home to stake a claim, my hand
no longer wore the size-five wedding band
inscribed to me from you, for I had sold
the yellow metal for scrap value and
reset one stone in a pendant of white gold.
Astounded that your wife could be so bold,
you muttered utter anguish. Undeterred
I loosed the pain too long restrained, untold,
then showed you out without another word.
Door shut, my voice turned verse. I soon must choose
better from worse, which gems to use or lose.

SEEKING THE SPHERES
By Rebecca Taksel

"Oh, Merlin," cries the King Arthur of *Camelot* on the eve of his certain military defeat and the death of all his dreams, "please don't let me die bewildered!" It is all he asks of the great magician who has guided him through his illustrious but tormented life. As I have moved through my middle years, I have become less bewildered. That is all I can claim, but I am immeasurably grateful to claim it.

On a gray, calm autumn day in one of the lakeside towns just north of Chicago, I sat on a boulder looking out over the blue-gray waters of Lake Michigan. I was in my forties, and I had been an alcoholic for all of my adult life. It was getting worse, as it always does. Every evening was a blank, every work day was filled with devious plans for lunchtime drinks and early quitting time. The thought of not drinking terrified me, but the people closest to me were warning me that I was a danger to myself and to others. I was wrecking my relationships, I was losing my grip at work, I was driving drunk.

On this day—I don't remember how I came to be at the lake—I was numb with misery, my mind stupefied, blank. I just sat, looking out into the gray expanse of water and clouds, for a minute, or five, or twenty. Suddenly, out of my mouth came the words, "Help me."

I had not *thought* the words in the usual sense. They spoke themselves *for me*, addressed themselves to the great empty spaces into which I had been gazing. Once spoken, I let them echo in my mind. I still wasn't thinking, but now I was part of the calm and quiet around me, above me. I had let go, let myself be lost in the vastness around me. I was, in a word, humbled.

I had had a dream a few nights before, in which I was floating free of the earth in a heavy, black night full of high winds. Then, somewhere out of the void, above the sound of the winds, I heard a voice. It was not a human voice but seemed to be the sound of the movement of the universe itself. At that moment of the dream I sensed that I had entered a state between life and death.

When I awoke I knew—and the knowledge grew over the next few days—that I was at a point where I must choose whether to live or die. Choosing to continue drinking was choosing to die. It was that simple. By the time I found myself at the water's edge, I was infused with this knowledge.

Later, after I had made the call to AA, after I had found a wonderful early-morning weekday meeting and had told my story, one of the members, a former minister, told me that I had experienced one of the manifestations of God, called by the Hebrews *ruah*. I don't know. I do know that the next three months, AA's "ninety meetings in ninety days," put me on the path to recovery. I never had a drink again; I was never seriously tempted. During my ninety days, members of AA warned me that the combination of peace and elation I felt was the "honeymoon" stage of sobriety. But it never really ended, and I can still almost conjure up that strange moment of letting myself go and trusting myself to float on water and air.

Still, it's fair to ask what happens to someone after what theologians and psychologists alike refer to as a conversion experience. In my forties, I didn't know what it might mean beyond salvaging my life on a practical level. I remember how ridiculously happy I was, for example, to accept a part-time job teaching in the evenings. I had not been able to work in the evening for so many years; evenings had been dedicated to drinking.

Gradually I realized that, while no clear path had been laid out for me, a way of walking the path that was my life, that was *life*, had been given to me. My marriage didn't survive, I suffered other reverses. But I was less bewildered. I was able, at a very low point, to know that more work was required, that I had once again to strip myself of all the comforts and illusions of daily life and find the humility I had felt at the lake. I won't even say that I learned not to be afraid. It is a searing thing to throw yourself out of yourself and into the cosmos. But sometimes it must be done, as a cleansing, as a reminder of how terrifying and wonderful our life is on our green and blue planet.

In the weeks following my initiation into sober living, I took a lot of walks. In my neighborhood was a large institution that served as a halfway house for mentally ill people. Some of them walked, too; and most of them were fine, enjoying the sunshine and passing clouds just as I did. But once in a while someone would be caught by the traps inside his mind, and he or she would fall into a pattern of frantic walking back and forth, or muttering of the same few phrases over and over again. Having been released from the cage of my own mind so recently, I could almost *see* the barbed wire that kept these people prisoners inside their own heads. Soon I realized that there were so many people walking around like that, people who, unlike the halfway house patients, were probably holding the keys to their own release. I had been given a key, and I promised in those early days to keep unlocking and unlocking chambers in my mind, however difficult it might be.

What do such keys unlock? Nothing mysterious really, just the realization that my life is *connected*. So many metaphors exist to explain this phenomenon, notably the "web" of being. It has become axiomatic in therapeutic literature that people need to connect with other people; those who do live longer and happier lives.

I found other important connections, too, as I began to follow stories about our growing knowledge of the intelligence and sensitivity of every sort of creature. As my knowledge grew, I could feel the strands of that web of life in a thousand ways every day.

Other connections were more interior, such as my growing ability to inhabit myself as a person with a history. I read recently that those of us who see our lives not as monoliths but as a series of different periods tend to do better psychologically in later life. Yes, I thought, I do see my life as a building with rooms added in stages. I have built a house, a ramshackle one perhaps, in which all the selves I was can now settle down together and learn from each other. This is only one metaphor for the richness of life and memory that so many people experience, especially as they grow older.

Finally, there are those connections that are ineffable, the ones that may manifest themselves as shooting stars in a dark night or as the quiet spinning of a silken thread. When I remember to look into the night sky I am still sometimes thrust out to the farthest reaches of my world, but I am not fearful. At such moments I often think of Walt Whitman's noiseless, patient spider, who "marked how to explore the vacant vast surrounding" as it "launched forth filament, filament, filament, out of itself." And I think of Whitman himself, the noiseless, patient observer of this tiny creature, who saw in the spider the image of his own soul, "surrounded, detached, in measureless oceans of space," ever "throwing, seeking the spheres to connect them . . ."

CARPE DIEM
By Alina Zeng

Every moment of our life marks a mission to achieve a goal, to keep a promise, to fulfill a dream. Dreaming of what could be is jumping into the midst of the sea, yet knowing the risks of perils ahead, even drowning, causes doubts deep within our minds to multiply. Still, we must try and swim through strong currents, through crackling storms, through bittersweet songs of the Sirens'. Maybe we will wash up on the wrong shore; maybe it will take us longer than expected to reach the end of our journey; or maybe we will turn back, at last. But maybe, we will find our way to where the waves calm and lap the warm sand, to where the breeze blows and brushes our skin, to where the children giggle and build their castles. We will live and love what we do, not just survive, allowing minutes to pass. At least we know... we have jumped off into the sea, and our lives now ring with possibility--more goals, more promises, and more dreams.

I KNOW THAT I KNOW
By Constance Gilbert

From personal experience and as a nurse, I believe we know our bodies well; therefore, we also realize when something is not right. We may not understand what it is, but we recognize the symptoms a physician needs to diagnose or order the tests to determine the cause.

I always tell my doctors to remember that even though I am a nurse, my body has not read the textbook. Yet I do know when changes occur. "Please listen to me."

In 1977, he did. A CAT scan identified a uterine fibroid tumor. My doctor said we'll keep an eye on it. Lots of woman have fibroids and live with them for years.

But I was feeling worse every day. He blamed it my hormones, which made some sense. Same answer next visit. Within a few more weeks I was miserable: nauseated, achy all over, depressed, fatigued, and rapidly gaining weight. He ordered an antidepressant. He was no longer listening just relying on the CAT scan results.

The morning I could no longer fit into my jeans, I phoned the gynecologist. The tumor had grown significantly. A hysterectomy was scheduled.

I was only 33 years old, a part-time nurse, a single mother with an eight-year-old son, and I was walking like a pregnant woman. I could not get comfortable due to the pelvic pressure.

Every evening, I crossed off that day on the calendar. *One day closer... I'll make it.*

One week prior to surgery, the gynecology office phoned to reschedule. My surgeon would be out of town. Now rescheduling an elective surgery is not uncommon. So the receptionist was not prepared for my response. "No, I won't make it that long!" I yelled. She tried to offer some alternatives. I would accept none of them.

Finally, after several conversations with the doctors, she said my doctor would do the surgery before flying to his conference, but his partner would have to care for me at the hospital. I agreed. "However, I'll never be able to get you on the surgery schedule; they are booked solid," the receptionist said.

Taking a deep breath, I quietly asked her to put me on hold one more time and try to schedule it. While I waited, I prayed with an intensity that surprised me. I did not know why, but I knew it was a life or death matter. Surgery could not be delayed.

Back on line, the receptionist said, "Somebody's looking out for you! A gallbladder surgery was cancelled seconds before I called." I thanked her and praised God for His intervention.

Three days earlier than the original date, I went to surgery. The evening before, I attended a hymn sing-a-long. A teenager had requested "Victory in Jesus." The second verse tells of His healing power and it encouraged me and gave me peace. As they wheeled me into the surgical suite, I was humming:

> *I heard about His healing,*
> *Of His cleansing pow'r revealing.*
> *How He made the lame to walk again*
> *And caused the blind to see;*
> *And then I cried, "Dear Jesus,*
> *Come and heal my broken spirit,"*
> *And somehow Jesus came and bro't*
> *To me the victory.*

Hours later I woke up in the recovery room singing the same song and knew that I had been healed. At that point I did not know the rest of the story, but I was content and went back to sleep.

Once they tapered down the pain medications, my doctor's partner came in and introduced himself. "First, I want you to know I assisted with your surgery. The tumor was large- the size of a baby's head, but benign. Second, I need to ask, 'How did you know the surgery could not be delayed?'"

"As a nurse, I have often known something was wrong with a patient when no one else did. I would just know... deep inside... I would know without a doubt. This time it was me. I knew I would die without the surgery and that it had to be done quickly. Not logical when it was "just" a fibroid. But I knew I wouldn't make it if we waited."

The surgeon's kind, deep brown eyes were on me, but I could tell that his mind was trying to comprehend what I meant. I waited.

Quietly, but with intensity he said, "Thank God, because you indeed would have died. Have you wondered why you've been sedated for three days?" (I did not know that I had lost three days.) He went on to explain the difficulty of the surgery, the inability to save the uterus and the details of a second tumor- the size of a large grapefruit- on my left ovary. It had ruptured as they were removing it. Had I not been in surgery at that specific time, I would have hemorrhaged and died within minutes.

I hummed "Victory in Jesus" as I praised the Great Physician for saving my life. God had allowed the skills of the physicians to heal me, but God had moved up the timetable. He knew about the second tumor and that it was bleeding within itself like a bomb primed to go off. He knew that the hormone imbalance was causing the fibroid to grow rapidly. God also knew the need for three surgeons instead of two, and an anesthesiologist instead of a nurse anesthetist. Yes, God had everything under control including the peace I felt through that old hymn I kept humming.

It still is one of my favorite hymns. Knowing He remains in control, I remain content.

RELIEF
By Aashna Belenje

Before boarding the plane,
I shivered under stormy skies,
My mind storming as much
With worrying about friends
And grades and grandparents,
So far away, too weak to fly
From India. Now we were
Taking a Christmas trip even
Farther from them to Maui;
And I knew, though I needed
A break, my worries would
Remain circling in my head.

A week later, I found myself
Sitting seaside with my family,
Turquoise waves calming me
Like nothing else had before.
Near sunset, the sky glowed
In pink, gold, orange, and hints
Of red, hues of a mystic dream
Setting waves afire and filling
My world with promise that
All would work out. As sea
Swallowed sun, I understood,
At last, the beauty of endings.

A STRONG REBIRTH
By Daawy

Every hairdresser who ever washed and blow-dried my hair felt the bump on my head, which was fortunately veiled beneath my dark strands. "An accident?" they would often question, for it was too intriguing for them to ignore its cause and thus my story commenced.

The car I was riding spun in the air, rotating several times before it pounded the ground. What was meant to be a blissful holiday spent in the farm resulted in my nanny's death — she jumped out of the car — my father's coma, my head being cut open, and breaking a limb. I was a toddler, but I still remember the incidents that followed vaguely. "How old were you?" the hairdressers from the diverse salons persisted.

"Not more than three." At such a young age, what we actually remember is often painted with scenes described by other people — in this case, family members. My sister who is two years my senior, for example, often recounted the sounds of the sirens approaching before the ambulance whisked us to the hospital. She also remembered the fierce red between her fingers as she realized that blood coated them like a sticky cobweb. My aunt reminisced of a relative covering my nanny's corpse with his white turban. I could not recall these disturbing imageries, since my injuries and that of Dad have surpassed that of the remaining passengers. He fell into a coma, while I was blanked out.

My mother told me years later, "You were lucky. The accident occurred during the Kuwait and Iraq war, so a skilled doctor from America was around to stitch the open wound on your head."

I smiled at her. My strong mother always managed to grasp the remnants of hope that shone brightly at the end of a tunnel with both hands. It was a trait I proudly inherited from her and compensated us both for our poor sense of direction. She was behind the wheels during that dreadful accident and my father was right beside her.

What I actually could still recall was Dad sleeping on a hospital bed in Germany. My sister and I spent hours customizing the 'Get Well Soon' cards he received during our visits. A classical piano occupied the vast living room in our accommodation. I sported a pink raincoat with two large pockets, each one portraying a picture of Precious Moments' caricatures, whilst my sister was shielded beneath a shiny red raincoat from the heavy rain. When my father could finally walk again, he would take us out for strolls, while we wrapped our small hands around his large thumb. I felt that Germany's relentless winds swore to make me soar along with my umbrella, no matter how firmly I held its latch. Hence my young mind could recollect the events that progressed through the trauma, which was mostly during the therapeutic stage, as opposed to the actual accident.

As I grew older, I became much more aware of my mother's strength. She was in her early twenties, and had to witness her family's anguish quietly, harboring the guilt even if it was never her fault. Her beloved husband slept with broken limbs on a bed, whilst she pleaded God to spare his life. Her children who did not yet surpass the age of five had to endure the aftermath of a car crash at such a young age. It was like riding a rollercoaster that collapsed. The childish songs we chanted in the car on our way to the farm were hastily replaced with screams. She had also lost our nanny for good. No matter how much I tried to liberate her confounded shock and pain through my words, I know now I would never be able to bring her feelings justice. Although the price my mother paid was high, for she never rode a vehicle again, she still held her family firmly. Not once did I remember tears gleaming from her pretty face and despite the turmoil, I only recall us laughing by Dad's bedside, our art that embellished the hospital's wall, our failed attempts at weaving a classical piano song and our walks together.

As an intense child, awful memories resided in my mind, no matter how hard I tried to shut them out. Friends and relatives often expressed their surprise whenever I detailed incidents that have occurred years ago. Therefore, I was certain that my strong, yet sensitive mother managed to conceal in front of us how broken she actually felt after the car crash. As a mother of four myself, and older than Mom at that time, I knew I would never have been able to cope the way she did. My silent tears would have constantly drenched my face, causing my children to panic. Sometimes dreadful accidents occur to demonstrate the true colors of those around us and I believe that my mother would never forget the people who did not point blaming fingers at her and supported her during her fall. It also solidified the bond between her and Dad. We were fortunate to have escaped death, for it was not yet our time and more blessed to have Mom as our mother.

SMILING FROM ABOVE
By Lynn C. Johnston

I stare into the twilight
And feel the shadows creeping near
But the darkness won't envelope me
For this I have no fear

His light will shine upon me
And for His guidance I will pray
As I join him in the Kingdom
Of that ever-lasting day

His arms will open wide
And encircle me with love
As I continue on my journey
Smiling from above

JOURNEY
By Judith Lyn Sutton

Deep inside
I plummet
On a bullet train
Of feelings:
Fear, the engine,
Grief, the next car
Third, guilt,
Fourth, despair.

Suddenly,
I become aware
Of rumbling –
A phrase, a line
Again and again
Until I know
To stop the diesel
I must begin,

Take my pen,
Scrawl the verse
And let it spin
Across the page,
Signaling
The dark cars
To take a side track
On thin blue rails.

Departure:
Station Loneliness;
Arrival:
Station Share,
I write from woe
To wonder
In poems
From there to here.

THE WRITING THAT SHAPED MY LIFE
By Diana Raab, Ph.D.

When I was ten years old, I found my grandmother dead in her room, which was right next to mine. On that sunny summer morning, I had knocked on her door to ask permission to swim in a friend's pool. I called her name, but she just lay in her bed beside the window, remaining perfectly still. On her stomach sat an opened Graham Greene book and a pair of eyeglasses. I touched her face and it was stone-cold. With a child's intuition, I sensed that something was seriously wrong. I ran out of the room to phone my mother at work.

Within minutes, emergency vehicles lined our once-quiet residential street. I remember two uniformed men carrying my grandmother out on a stretcher down the creaky wooden stairs. I prayed they wouldn't drop her.

After the commotion of ambulances, paramedics, and my parents frantically rushing about simmered down, the grief of my loss penetrated me like a deep-seated bullet. My true healing only began days later when my mother handed me my first journal—one with Khalil Gibran quotes at the top of each page—and told me to pour my grief onto its pages. Little did my mother know that her seemingly benign gesture set the stage for my work as a writer. In other words, that traumatic event transformed me and guided me during many years of my life. Since then, I've used writing as a form of healing, and teach others to do the same.

There wasn't much talk about my grandmother until about twenty years after her death, when my parents were getting ready to move from my childhood home in Queens, New York. While packing, they stumbled across my grandmother's retrospective journal, which she'd written after emigrating from Vienna in the early 1930s. Only after reading that document did I truly understand the deep roots of her depression, which tormented her for her entire life, and eventually led to her suicide at the age of sixty-one. I also realized how we carry a lot in our DNA, and my desire to write probably originated from my beloved grandmother.

I tucked her journal away, then pulled it out again when I was diagnosed with breast cancer at the age of forty-seven. In addition to wanting to figure out if my grandmother had taken her life due to a breast-cancer diagnosis and surgery, I wanted to become inspired by her words so I could write my own story.

During the days following my surgery, I lay in a hospital bed surrounded by orchids sent by loved ones around the country. Tear-saturated tissues lay piled high on my bedside table, and the early-morning sun peaked through the large window in my room. The emotional pain of losing a breast hit me hard. When my surgeon said he would soon remove the corset-like bandage wrapped tightly around my chest, I feared seeing what lay beneath. What would be the new condition of one of the breasts that had nursed my three now-teenage children?

Just days after my surgery, my husband reached out across the sterile white bed sheets to take my hand. Simon, an engineer and natural-born "fixer," had a difficult time watching me endure intense physical and emotional pain. He nestled up close to me and wrapped both his hands around mine. He looked deeply into my eyes, as he had years earlier on the day of my father's passing.

"Right now," he asked, "if you could do one thing that would make you happy, what would that be?" Aside from being guaranteed a long life and watching my children have children, I said I wanted to return to school for a master's degree in writing. For years, this had been a dream of mine, and the recent surgery suddenly slapped me face-to-face with my own mortality and my apparent race against time. I wanted this dream to come true.

When I was navigating difficult times, my writing mentor at Spalding University repeatedly told me, "When it hurts, write harder." As a result, during the years of my breast-cancer journey, my journal became the forum for venting my fears and frustrations. Eventually parts of my journal entries ended up in my self-help memoir, *Healing with Words: A Writer's Cancer Journey*. The book not only helped me, but assisted others in navigating their own healing journeys.

Ever since that day during my childhood when my mother gave me my first journal, I had always found solace in the written word. Journaling became a passion that I turned to during turbulent times—from my own adolescence, to difficult pregnancies, and finally during my two bouts with cancer.

My writing didn't stop with my MFA in writing. I continued to journal and write, as this has always been my life's calling. Six years after my breast-cancer diagnosis, I was diagnosed with multiple myeloma, a rare and incurable form of bone-marrow cancer most often seen in men exposed to toxic chemicals. I continued to be a medical mystery and challenge for my doctors. Once again, I turned to my journals to chronicle my journey, which included numerous travels and medical opinions. Woven into my accounts were my sentiments about my ongoing zest for life, and my desire to not be categorized as "a cancer patient," in spite of the diagnosis. I realized the ongoing importance of following my passions and living out my dreams.

As a sixtieth birthday present to myself, I returned to school to get my Ph.D. in transpersonal psychology. My dissertation dealt with how other published writers had been healed and transformed through writing, and the results were powerful. Thus, I can truly say that writing has saved my life, as well as the lives of many other creative individuals.

Over the years I've learned that when in distress, many people turn to writing because it empowers them and helps them heal. We can say that when life takes an unexpected turn, journals can become our best friends. Poet Langston Hughes said, "When I feel bad, I write in order to keep from feeling worse."

Writing to feel better is probably the most common reason why people crack open their journals. Therapists often suggest journaling as a part of the healing process to help channel problems. Poet Kim Stafford once said that the journal lets him wallow, if that's what he needs. "But," he said, "the act of writing lifts me out."

During my own early life, the journal my mother gave me to help me cope with my grandmother's suicide helped me come to peace with my loss. The journal became my best friend and confidant, especially when there was no one else to talk to. The challenges surrounding illness can also become a catalyst for journaling.

Writing has been a healthy habit for me, just like brushing my teeth or meditating. For the writer, the journal or notebook is not only a place to play around with words and voice; it's a place to foster a more intimate relationship with who we are. The journal is also a place to gather momentum and excitement about writing, akin to an artist's sketchbook.

Many writers, including myself, use their journals as catchalls for personal experiences and observations and as seeds for future works. In fact, the beginnings of all my books have begun on the pages of my journal. There's something about the creative impulse that arises when one has a pen and journal in hand that is sometimes difficult to replicate on a computer.

As I think back to all that has occurred in my life and all the experiences I've both enjoyed and endured, I must give heartfelt thanks to my mother for knowing that I needed an outlet for my turbulent emotions at the tender age of ten . . . and giving me the Khalil Gibran journal that ultimately helped me save my own life.

MAYA ANGELOU, AN ANGEL OF HEALING
By F. Anthony D'Alessandro

My vacation hospital visit wasn't planned. Hearing my groans and observing my discomfort on a cruise ship, my wife asked a local cab driver to rush me to the nearest Bahamian medical complex.

After finding a wrinkled wooden chair in the pint-sized hospital waiting room we sat anticipating a quick visit with a doctor. Twenty-five scattered patients assembled in front of and around us. After a hapless four-hour wait at the island's local hospital, only one person entered the doctor's office for treatment. We scrambled back to our ship. The next day our cruise ship set sail for home. We decided that I'd secure admission at a medical center in my Celebration hometown soon after disembarking.

This all seems like a scramble in my mind today. The last time I'd been involved in a hospital stay, the Brooklyn Dodgers dominated the National League. At the time, zealous interns tackled me. I struggled to run away and I felt as elusive as my speedy as Dodger hero Robinson. Medics in white garb sought to stab the 12-year-old me with some anti-rabies vaccine. I escaped. Fortunately, after a few hours of searching, they captured the dog who'd snacked on my leg. Testing declared him rabies free.

Now, three score years later, I entered in a hospital once again. This time, I was aching and anxious to get the attention of any medical professionals. After three days in intensive care, I felt poked like a dartboard by numerous chilled claws. Fortunately, I healed. Medically pardoned, my caretakers released me. A small army of doctors and nurses came by to help support me during my stay. Despite healing touches, I found it easy to grumble. Two nurses in particular stood by me every day. I whined about their Dracula-like thirst for taking out too much blood and could feel their icy hands clamped and ready to tap for more, at any hour. They managed, however, to attend to my every medical need.

These nurses seemed polite and sensitive. They cared for me throughout my stay. One nurse, a lean volleyball player looking type, did not appreciate my banter. Stone-faced, one of my wisecracks alarmed her into rallying her troops and bullying me into taking an MRI test. As her devoted posse raced me to that isolation machine, I felt like an Olympic luge sledded cutting corners, bouncing off walls. Finally, this sled where I sat saddled, stopped abruptly, and launched me into the glass mini Chunnel for the test. All of those comforting church bell sounds that I'd heard earlier, just a short distance from my room, faded into that cluttered night, and were ultimately swallowed up by that sealed isolation tube wrapped all around me.

I passed that MRI Test. Sadly, the reason for my taking it was a result of my nonsensical comments. My bizarre behavior prompted the dedicated boss nurse into commandeering her loyal luge mates to rocket me into the testing tunnel.

I'd learned my lesson in obedience. I became more obedient than a Trappist monk. For the next two days, I remained courteous, yet "cool" toward these dedicated women. They provided the necessary services for my survival and legitimate escape. I limited my responses to "yes" and "no" answers. Still, I considered the nurses somewhat soulless, aloof, and all-business.

On my last day before dismissal, I read aloud from my internet connection, "Dr. Maya Angelou passed away." The pair of nurses in my room froze. The Luge traffic director stopped, strolled over, and stopped in front of me. To my surprise, medical chatter was not on her mind. She whispered tearfully, "I knew Maya Angelou. I wish that you had not read that." My other nurse wandered around the room, head down wearing a sort of hang dog look, while simultaneously wiping her eyes with the back of her right hand.

There are times when one deservedly earns the crown of, "Total Jerk." I'd just experienced that moment. The taller woman, whom I'd resented for days, quivered and looked deeply into my eyes as she spoke. "I was in college working as a waitress in a local eatery. I served Maya. She offered me her business card, autograph, and some other memorabilia. Ms. Angelou invited me to sit at her dining table. She then encouraged me to become a doctor, noting that she would be glad to speak to medical school personnel at her university on my behalf." For once, my mouth remained shut. Then, to my surprise, my lower lip began quivering. In fact, the muscular room, stuffed and sprouting with medical machinery appeared eerily silent and still. The introduction of Maya Angelou into the conversation tamed my foolishness and humanized those nurses. Instantly, I felt genuine affection and respect toward these committed hospital professionals. When they left, I ambled into an obscure corner of my room. I felt the weight of guilt for my initial mean-spirited reaction toward these healers. Thoughts and memories of Maya Angelou captured my moment. I'd found Angelou's writing upbeat and inspirational. On the day I'd read about her passing, her magic appeared to trickle into the hospital room. I reflected on her poetry. One of her quotes boomed across my brain, "Try to be a rainbow in someone's cloud." That room seemed brighter as I sensed the angelic presence of the wondrous poet pause and stop in to pay a visit.

This poet's passing prompted me to look at people with a clearer, fairer vision, to give, to forgive, to understand others and to thank God for sending these nurses my way to heal my ailments.

A LIFE IN 5 MINUTES
By Juley Harvey

life
really does
that flashing thing
before your eyes,
as you prepare
to evacuate,
running before fire, flood,
everything coming at you,
all your life that was,
stormy villains coming
to get you, to take you away, haha,
in a hail of blazing, swimming fury,
bullets of flame and mud.
you go against the current,
the grain, the fuel, everything,
what? remembering
that darned checklist of what to take
with you in an emergency.
and what do you come up with?
the need for speed?
no, an unbearable desire for cookies,
a cookie fix,
never mind the lifesaving prescriptions
oh, and all the people
that go with all the memories
of all the things
you're abandoning
and those you have to try to
whisk up in the allotted 5 minutes.
no 15 minutes of fame here.
you'll probably wind up
with a bunch of doh-doh
doodads and no socks

that match,
but at least you'll always
have that note from a boy in the sixth grade
you haven't thought of
in years;
you'll always have wherever-it-is.
not exactly Paris,
not exactly bogey,
but some swagger, nonetheless.
but matching socks? a toothbrush?
your 93-year-old father's oxygen machine?
a pox!
we are emblazoned, emboldened
by a furnace of muddy flood.
we need a bigger ark — too much stuff to park
and too many outings — hark!
"we're on fire now!" and "a flood of memories"
flame with surging, purging, urgent meanings,
dug from the bright deep,
our souls to keep.
as long as we remember
ourselves, each other,
our family fur babies,
we are not doomed,
we can still breathe,
there is room
among the ruinous spilt tears
both to leave
and to stretch and grow,
grab our remembered bootstraps
and go on again.
we emerge heroes,
from the other side
of fire and flood,
seared, bathed in
tears, sweat, and blood.
perhaps we're not miraculous
by nature, necessarily,
but that's something
we can seem to be,
brave, impossible evacuee,
waving the bright flag
of moment and mortality.
5 minutes to decide

what your life looks like,
the roadmap to future
from past,
what has weight, value,
eternal meaning, gold from chaff,
sifting ash
from shifting wind,
grabbing glory
from grubby mud,
wailing waters,
watching, watching
as firecloud, fireline,
floodline and tide
approach, encroach,
packing punches
and bad horror stories,
helpless, helpless,
until the heroic helicopters
and mighty tankers swoop and dip
their saving grace and rain,
drop their zip lines,
open their mouths
for safe passage —
"come in," they said,
"well we'll give you shelter
from the storm,"
as bob dylan once sang.
shelter we found
in each other,
rainbows in
our backyards.
even in the infamous
"no flush zone,"
after the flood,
which offered its own
carols and lessons
and testaments
to human ingenuity,
if not dignity,
especially when
the friendly neighborhood port-a-potties
went tilt
in the winds,
and citizens in need

trudged through the night
with flashlight and robe,
searching for honest relief
and perhaps some toilet paper.
and hope. always hope.
which was there,
though sometimes in
a good disguise.
you've got to give it
to nature;
and she's giving it to us.
all those critters,
for all those years,
going in the woods.
who knew
indoor plumbing
is a cause
to party and rejoice?
it all boils down to
bare simplicity.
the choice?
in fire and flood,
save what matters,
use your voice
for the earth,
before it ends
in ash and splatters.
fire and ice? maybe not.
but the fire and rain
came.
a lot.
and we ran
before them,
seeking safe haven,
evacuees remembering
the blessings
of the storm.

I WANT YOU TO LEAVE
By Cona Faye Gregory-Adams

I wrote the following poem after my brother had received the news that he was facing lung cancer and a tumor on the brain. He had made the decision to forego any further treatment, including surgery. My sisters and I knew that he had voluntarily given himself a death sentence.

LOSS OF A BROTHER

I am eighteen months,
to the day,
younger than he.

We have two sisters,
both younger than we.

To lose our only brother
leaves three sisters
cast adrift in a head sea,
swamped in waves
breaking tight
against the course
of our ship, poised -

to grow old together,
reminiscing,
laughing about the past.

Yet he longs to be free.
We are left with no choice,
but to step aside,
and allow him leave.

We live in Missouri, but one sister lives in Wyoming. She flew home as soon as she heard about his decision, but gave us the news that she could not come again for the funeral. She stated that since she is losing her eyesight, flying has become very difficult for her, and she had wanted to visit with him while he was still alive.

Our brother, Elman Gregory, had been on oxygen for 15 years. He had suffered from emphysema, a collapsed lung, and lung surgery. Now he was facing further lung problems and a new tumor in the brain. When given the news that more surgery could easily necessitate the use of a ventilator, from which he might never be released, he made a difficult choice; no more tests, no surgery.

We knew that the time left to him would be short. He had always participated in pool, volleyball, and water skiing during his weekends and vacations. He had many friends and enjoyed an active social life, even after the addition of oxygen, installing a pool table in his basement. The "guys" came over for pool three times a week. Friends continued to get together for a meal once a month, taking turns with preparation. They simply switched location of the dinners to my brother's house instead of rotating among the group.

He continued to drive, shop, eat out, and attend family events, using a portable oxygen supply. He enjoyed inviting his extended family out to his favorite pizza restaurant, where he bought everyone dinner. He had a great sense of humor, and often kept us laughing with his quick wit.

TAKING CHANCES

He was the eldest, tall, handsome,
all knowing (by his own assessment).

He could roll a 'guide and wheel'
to school, without a stop. That wheel
kept rolling as if by magic.
He could shimmy up a tree in search
of wild grapes. swim in deep water,
or catch snakes for pets.

He could hunt squirrels with Dad,
shoot a 22 rifle, and bring dinner home.
He could milk a cow, 'slop' the hogs,
or hitch a horse to the wagon.

He could zing you, square on
with a dry dirt clod or corn cob.
He could run barefoot through woods,
creeks, fields, and over dirt roads.

But he missed the rafter, fell through
to the floor below, knocked himself out cold,
chasing his cat through the attic.

He backed off a second floor,
with no stair rail, and fell
straight down to the ground floor.

He ran across the back porch
to slide on a board placed at the end,
slipped, and knocked himself out again.

He pulled the wagon downhill, and
found himself pinned to the corn crib
by the runaway wagon's long tongue.

He married three women,
struck out three times.

Yet he served in the U. S. Navy,
worked on the flight deck,
kept his motorcycle onboard,
and explored every port,
without a scratch.

After his decision to accept no further treatment, he began to make difficult end-of-life decisions, one of which included marrying his long-time girlfriend, Carol, who had currently moved in to take care of him. During his last weeks, both my sister, Linda, and I cooked some of his favorites and spent time in his home to visit with him. His appetite had abated, but we tempted him with lemon pie, fried chicken, pecan pie, bacon and eggs, etc.

Hospice had been called in, and had given us the news that the final week had arrived. We were told on Monday that my brother could "go at any moment," and by Friday the end would come. My sister and I had been taking turns spending the night. At this news from the hospice nurse, we decided to stay.

After the nurse left, Elman's new wife said, "I want you to leave."

Linda and I were stunned. "Why?" we asked.

"I want to be alone with him," she said. "I deserve to be alone with him."

"Carol, our brother is dying, and you want us to leave?" we said. "We are not leaving."

Carol stormed into her room and slammed the door.

I called my husband, Bill. "Could you please come over and talk to Carol? She's asking us to leave." I said. I told him what the hospice nurse had said. "We want to stay with him. Perhaps if you talk to her, or maybe pray with her, she will be reasonable."

Bill came. He and Carol walked into her bedroom and closed the door. After a few minutes, they came out. She walked back into Elman's room and closed the door. Bill came into the living room. "It's okay. You can stay," he said.

Later, when I asked Bill what he had said to change Carol's mind, he said he asked her if she was planning to murder Elman.

"Oh, no. I would never do that," she said.

"Think about how your behavior appears to others," he said. "If we are compelled to force the issue, I'm sure the Sheriff would naturally come to the conclusion that you want to be alone with him in order to hasten his death."

After Bill left, Carol apologized. She then proceeded to keep the door to Elman's room closed, and would allow us only a few minutes at a time in the room with him. By Wednesday, he had lapsed into a coma.

"Linda, we are going to sing to him," I said.

"We can't do that," she said.

"Of course, we can," I said. "We need to do this. I've heard the last thing to go is hearing."

"My voice is too low," she said.

"Okay," I said. "You sing Alto and I'll sing Soprano. He doesn't even know we are here. He needs to know we're here."

Reluctantly, Linda agreed. The next time Carol allowed us in my brother's room, Linda stood on one side of his bed, and I stood on the other. I took hold of one of his hands while Linda held the other. We sang familiar hymns, the words of which we had committed to memory as a result of a lifetime spent taking part in congregational singing in church.

"Well, that would make me want to die real fast," Linda said as we left Elman's room. I knew we weren't virtuosos, but at the point of death, intent carries the greater weight. I know that he heard us sing the hymns. He gave Linda's hand a slight squeeze. We sang to him again on Thursday. On Friday, he took his last breath. Fortunately for us, Carol did allow us a few minutes in the room with him afterward.

DEATH'S GENTLE SIGH

His body still warm,
our brother lay still,
his face set in perfect repose,
the echo of our voices
lifted in hymn, fading
like the rattle of death
in those closing days
before the last soft breath.

I wanted to watch his spirit rise,
reaching upward toward
the prize his faith had earned.
I had to be content
with a tender touch
and unspoken words of farewell,
bathed in tears of longing
to share his final journey.

    I do miss my brother. We were only 18 months apart in age, and enjoyed an amiable relationship. I admired and respected him. Yet I have no regrets about my part in the circumstances surrounding his passing. I know that he met death on his own terms and he was ready to go when the moment came. I wrote many poems about him while he lived, and several more during and after his passing. Writing about him has clarified my feelings, deepened my appreciation of his unique character, and lessened my grief. I anticipate a happy reunion when it's my turn to go.

THE NIGHT BREEZE
By Lynn C. Johnston

In the quiet stillness of the night
A breeze gently stirs the leaves on the trees
And your memory drifts into my mind
You are with me once again
I can almost smell your sweet scent lingering in the air
And feel your touch brushing softly against my skin
I close my eyes and see your beautiful face looking at mine
With a smile that treats my wounded heart with a healing salve
If only I could press your lips to mine one more time
And hear your voice that keeps playing in my mind
Like a favorite song I never want to end
Did I just hear you giggle or was it my imagination?
Oh, how I miss hearing your laugh
I know you'll have to leave soon, but please stay with me
Until my eyes grows weary and I can no longer fight sleep
Then I will look forward to another evening
When the night breeze will return you to me
And we can be together once more

FRESHMAN TRYOUT
By Carol J. Rhodes

Once-a-week lessons for over a year, plus practice for two hours every day, rain or shine, were about to pay off. Very early one hot, humid Saturday morning in mid-May, seventeen hopefuls assembled in the steamy high school gymnasium where the cheerleader auditions for the coming school year were about to begin.

Being the tallest and thinnest among the candidates, I admit having pangs of envy when I compared myself to the other girls there. All of them were in shorts and blouses tied at the midriff which showed off their cute, curvy figures. I was wearing a uniform I borrowed from a girl down the street who had been a cheerleader at another school.

"Maybe it will bring you good luck," Wanda Jean had said the day before as she folded over and pinned large pleats in the short skirt to make it fit my small waist. Sadly, the skirt hung limp and uneven against my body, instead of flaring out like it may have done on someone with fuller hips. The letter sweater was also too large, but we concluded it would take more than safety pin alterations to make it right. I was determined to wear it anyway. The wide tops of the short white leather boots I had saved my allowance for months to buy also accentuated my long broomstick legs.

Tension mounted as the hot sun filtered in through the windows high above us. Seated on bleachers, we waited for our turn to show what we could do. The girl next to me tapped her feet on the empty row in front of us, and repeatedly adjusted the rubber band holding her ponytail in place.

"Are you nervous?" I finally managed to ask. "Nah, piece of cake," was her flippant reply. Well, I certainly was nervous, even though I had worked hard on my routine and knew I had it down pat.

Performing with the first group, comprised of five girls, I was clearly the best. My cartwheels were perfect, my voice strong. I was even able to run, jump up high and land effortlessly in a split, while groans came from some of the competitors who attempted the same maneuver. The last group of girls to compete had been cheerleaders the previous year. As I watched them, I was confident my showing had been just as polished as theirs, if not more so.

I had dreamed of this moment for more than a year. I could just see myself and the other cheerleaders leading our football team onto the field, the crowd wild in anticipation of another victory. In a backdrop of stadium lights, I saw us perform intricate routines while leading the pep squad in all our favorite school cheers. Now my fantasies were about to come true.

With perspiration matting my hair in ringlets around my face, I finally gave in and pushed the sleeves of my sweater up above my elbows. Waiting for the results, everyone was surprisingly quiet. It was nearly noon before the head gym teacher, Mrs. Barnett, returned from her office, clipboard in hand, along with her two assistants who were there to assist in the selection.

"Girls, thank you all for coming this morning," Mrs. Barnett began. "Now, if I may have your attention, I will read the names of the lucky ones we have selected for the upcoming school year." At an agonizingly slow pace, she began to read the names from her list. I started to count on my fingers after I realized the names were not in alphabetical order. Seven down, three to go. Then two, then only one. As their names were called, the girls stood up and made their way down to the court.

Tears welling in my eyes, I counted the girls again, hoping one more name, mine, would be called. But there were already ten girls hugging one another and shrieking with excitement as they danced and pranced around the gym. Something told me I should stay and congratulate them, but at the moment I felt sick. All I wanted to do was to leave.

When I returned home, my mother met me at the door. "Well, how did it go?"

"We're not going to find out anything until next week, "I fibbed, but no doubt she must have seen the disappointed look on my face. I headed to my room where I stayed until suppertime.

"Today was the big day, right?" my dad asked after he said the blessing.

"Yeah."

Well, tell us all about it, for goodness sakes," he coaxed.

"I'm not feeling very good....it was so hot today.... I have a headache, and don't feel like talking right now," I managed to mumble. "Can I be excused, please?"

I dreaded having to tell my parents the truth, absolutely sure *they* had never suffered such a painful letdown. I missed seeing the knowing looks which must have passed between them.

After school the following Monday, I stopped by the gym teacher's office where she was busy trying to close a too-full drawer of her filing cabinet.

"Mrs. Barnett, could I speak with you a moment, please?"

"Yes, but make it quick. I'm late for a meeting."

"I just wanted to ask you why I wasn't picked," I said in a shaky voice. Without looking at me, she responded, "Well, I have to admit you were one of the better contestants, but I, I mean we, decided you're just too tall and skinny. You wouldn't have fit in, size-wise, with the others."

Later I reluctantly told my mother about the tryouts and my conversation with the gym teacher. Gathering me in her arms, she stroked my hair.

"You know, honey, all through your life, you're going to have disappointments. Learning how to deal with them is just part of growing up. Now after you change clothes, why don't you go on out in the yard and practice your cartwheels. A lot can change between now and next year's competition. In fact, I've heard Mrs. Barnett may be retiring."

For the first time, I let myself cry.

I've never forgotten this disappointment, or my mother's words. She was right.

I have experienced many other disappointments throughout the remainder of my school years, later in my career, and then in my love life. But things did change, mainly my attitude.

When viewing the disappointments I once thought would surely bring about the *end of the world*, I realize they were really not such *big deals* after all.

TWO WOMEN
By Judy Shepps Battle

It has been nineteen years since the deaths of two women who played key roles in my life -- my mother and my lover. Both birthed me, one biologically and the other as a proud and out lesbian. Both committed suicide after a lifetime of reluctant living.

Lillian, my mother, died of renal failure after 30 years of intermittent suicide attempts. She stopped eating and drinking and her kidneys failed. We were emotionally estranged all of my life, but I did get to spend time with her, make amends, and say good-bye.

She was 80 years old.

Elizabeth, my lover, after a lifetime of craving death died of a deliberate and self-inflicted drug overdose. She was a doctor -- an anesthesiologist -- who set up her own lethal IV leaving a note on the door saying "if you don't like dead bodies, don't come in."

After an intense seven months together, we had been estranged and so I never got to see the note. I also never got to say good-bye.

She had just celebrated her 33rd birthday.

Grieving

I am still grieving my loss of these two women. As connected as I was to both, I was unable to force either one to stay with me -- not in life and not in death.

Mourning was a skill never modeled in my growing-up family. We lived out a credo of denial and didn't talk, trust, or feel, let alone share our emotions. Despite this, I became a successful university professor and clinical psychotherapist. I also became an active addict and co-dependent.

I began to use food addictively as a preschooler, and added prescription drugs by late elementary school. Our family-owned pharmacy became my first supplier of narcotics with codeine-based cough syrup given for minor coughs and amphetamines for losing weight.

The familial code of silence taught full-blown co-dependent

skills. I became quite proficient at reading other people's needs and putting them before mine. Fear ruled my every step. I was terrified of the everyday unpredictable anger and emotional abuse; however, I was equally afraid to lose my family by telling our secrets to strangers.

Many of these dynamics were painfully repeated in my adult interactions with Lillian and Elizabeth.

It has taken many years for me to realize what powerful teachers both these women were -- and continue to be -- for me.

Lesson One: Trusting and Loving Myself

We each play a role in childhood.

Mine was to be an unobtrusive chameleon, adroitly determining the emotional needs of each family member and changing my psychological coloration to fit their perception of reality. When asked my opinion on anything, I first figured out what he or she was thinking and then supported their point of view. I knew it was critical that they not be upset with me.

As a young adult, I sought my own identity by opposing all family values. I was a free spirit and political radical in the 1960s, while my family basked in middle-class conservatism. I dated non-Jews, a cardinal sin in those days and major source of family embarrassment.

What I didn't know was that as long as I focused only on not becoming like them, I wasn't free to identify, create, and embrace my own belief and value system.

As an adult, I continually invested more love and trust in people, places, and things than I did in myself. I looked for people who could "complete me"; who could do the tasks I didn't trust myself to do; who could love me when I couldn't love myself. One by one -- whether from divorce, death, or disinterest -- these people disappeared.

I am left with only one person to trust and to be loved by -- myself.

The departures of Lillian and Elizabeth have driven home this awareness. I believe that their karmic role in my life was to unwaveringly refuse to meet my trust and love needs, so that I would eventually turn to myself as provider.

Lesson Two: Sharing Myself and Trusting the Universe

In my family, we were taught to hoard.

Lillian's outlook was based on a Great Depression model of scarcity. Food and money were stashed away. When I cleared out her apartment, Band-Aid boxes and other unlikely empty containers camouflaged five and ten dollar bills. Her cupboard held more cans of coffee and soup than could be consumed by a family of five in a year.

We also hoarded ourselves emotionally and spiritually.

"Outsiders" were seen as "leeches" (her favorite word) who would "drain us of our life blood and then walk away." I was caught between a rock (a non-giving family) and a hard place (dangerous outsiders).

I was scared to be with my family, and scared to leave them.

Elizabeth also felt unable to share herself fully with me. Despite her accomplishments in the medical field, she felt unworthy of my love because thought she had nothing of value to give back. I knew it was her depression talking but her prescribed medication and counseling sessions couldn't break through her belief that she was better off dead.

She spoke of her emotional pain as being a "parasite in her system," and believed that the only way to find relief was for the host (her) to die.

Elizabeth and Lillian taught me many life lessons but the biggest one is that no matter how despairing I become, taking my life is not an option. I could never inflict such trauma on my loved ones.

Becoming Whole

In my recovery from addiction and resultant spiritual explorations, I am learning the limitless abundance of the universe -- that my internal energy tank is replenished by sharing, rather than drained.

My teachers, Lillian and Elizabeth, both in life and in their death, taught me to trust my own instincts, to support what is healthy for me, to take gentle care of myself and others, and to freely share that self with others. Both women held up mirrors reflecting the toxic price of negativity.

It's much too high.

I truly wish my relationships with Lillian and Elizabeth could have had a storybook ending -- a deathbed conversion to hope and trust -- but the Author had something else in mind. My task is to continue to grow emotionally and spiritually so that the intergenerational cycle of addiction, co-dependency, and negativity ends with me.

BRIAN'S TREE
By Beckie A. Miller

Today should have been my son's forty-second birthday. Instead, as for the past twenty-four years, I stand barefoot among the grasses, tenderly caressing the silken needles of the pine tree planted in his memory so long ago seeing him as I last saw him – eighteen-years old. The tiny, brown pine cones scattered sparingly on the tips of its branches remind me of another time and the infant child once growing within my womb. Salty tears mingle with a tender smile — oh, so bittersweet!

Bitter memories entwine with sweet as I admire this tree. Its growth represents a circle of life. Brian's tree is now over twenty-feet tall, growing sturdily and beautiful as our son once grew. The irony of my thoughts does not escape me as I lightly caress a branch, desperately searching for the beauty — silent, invisible hope — among other branches. I search for it daily in my struggle to survive the endless sorrow of my aching heart. Sunlight streams through the spaces between each branch creating a special glow that matches my mood and yet, mocks it too.

Christmas of 1991 – six weeks after he was killed. What already seemed a lifetime of tears, shattered dreams, and horrific pain. You die of accident, illness, or aging. Brian did not simply die. He was murdered. Such a horrible word and yet no aesthetic sugar coating can erase it. No other word can do justice to the horrific reality. It was horrible what happened to our son, to us. We planted a tree that first Christmas without him. We knew nothing else to do to keep him close to our hearts, but through another living thing. Still in shock we did not yet fully realize the implications of living without him - the future profoundly changed - our emotional time stood still forever to become life "after Brian was killed."

We have carried on and the repercussions of his death have not left us totally filled with hate, despair, bitterness, or devoid of joy. I still believe in the overall good and beauty in life, even as simple as this tree. We were lucky, my family and I, to see much compassion from caring people in our lives and our neighborhood. Lucky seems an odd word to use when you have suffered the worst of life's humanity. Compassionate people, a side of tragic events that give us hope despite the darkness; the good that comes even out of evil. However, we hurt. We are angry at times. We anguish and suffer — like today. We always will.

As I bask in the warmth of the sun streaming through the branches reaching toward the heavens, I reflect on this tree in front of me. Strong roots give it life. The same as the cord attached to my infant son, giving him life once. A cord severed by birth — physically — but never emotionally. A mother's bond transplanted now in nurturing this representation of what once was in my life, now only in my heart. Growing and nurturing is what motherhood is about. This tree does not take his place and yet I water, feed, and relish the fact it is flourishing with my attentions despite the wrath of the desert's relentlessly scorching summers.

As Brian's tree flourishes, it reminds me I can too, in spite of a broken heart that will never heal; in spite of a family left behind like a jigsaw puzzle in pieces. We have put the puzzle together again with much diligence and hard work because of our commitment to each other to remaining whole, and yet, a part of us is missing. We can never piece it together completely and the road of grief we travel sometimes causes the pieces to become displaced again and again. What is left of the puzzle though is still a family. Family pictures are bittersweet reminders of this fact. We smile. We are three — Don, Christie, and me. A later family picture, Don, Christie, Kimberlie, and me, when five years after his murder, we adopted a baby girl. In our hearts and memories, though, we will always be one more than any picture shows.

"Hello, Brian's tree. You look beautiful today." Briefly during this conversation, I worry what someone passing might think — then realize — I don't care. I have earned my right: grief allows me the freedom to talk to myself and this tree. "Happy birthday, dearest son. Oh God, please let the magic of sweet memories of our life together and the beauty in this tree always console us. Thank you for allowing yet another anniversary to pass, not without pain — it never will — but simply without further trauma to my family and myself.

We went from being simply victims, as we survived by breathing and getting out of bed each morning. I wanted to not only survive my son's murder, but live life fully in spite of it. It was not an easy journey. With the adoption of our daughter, now nineteen-years old, we opened our hearts to love again, swallowing our fears and vulnerability. She taught us to laugh and awaken once more – to see the world through the innocence of a child - to allow our broken hearts to be renewed. Two grandsons born since, have added exponentially to our joy. I truly thought that joy was something I would never experience again, but I have experienced it even stronger than before as a result of enduring such incredible sorrow and the appreciation of coming out on the other side.

As I will inevitably stand on these grasses admiring this tree many more times; as love never ends, let this tree never die... I love you, Brian. May the same strong roots giving life to this tree, continue to give life to us.

Love always, Mom, Dad, your sisters, and nephews.

THE EAGLE HAS LANDED
By Edward Louis

"The Eagle has landed," I said confidently into the lobby telephone of a quiet Rio de Janeiro hotel. As I hung up, the desk clerk looked at me oddly.

"Just calling my wife," I nodded and began dragging my suitcase towards the elevator.

It was my safe arrival call back home – the importance of which had been drilled into me by my father as I was growing up.

It seemed I couldn't leave our property without hearing him bellow, "Call me when you get there." His desire to protect us was ever-present. "Watch where you're going" or "be careful with that" tripped off his tongue as easily as "hello."

As I grew up, got married and started my own family, I began to understand his need to know that nothing had harmed us when we were away from him. Life was good, but my job required me to do a lot of international traveling. Long flights, busy meetings and hotel rooms in foreign countries meant little time for me to watch over my family – or for my family to watch over me.

Before the advent of cell phones and email, personal communication from these locales was often inconvenient and always expensive. Instead of having a long telephone conversation relaying the day's events, a brief "safe arrival" call would have to suffice. I would call my wife, Wendy, and recite the famous words said by Neil Armstrong in 1969 during the Apollo 11 moon landing: "The Eagle has landed." With that simple phrase, she would know that I had gotten to my destination as planned and everything was okay.

As our kids grew up and moved away, she, too, would have her share of exotic travels – like to California to see our daughter or to Florida to visit our sons. No matter where she went, I could be assured of a safe arrival call with our signature phrase.

Over the years, we discussed the last trip either one of us would ever have to take – that trip to the "Great Beyond." We always said that the one who got there first needed to send back a sign that they had crossed over successfully – in essence, giving a "safe arrival" call.

More than 30 years later – and eight months after being diagnosed with pancreatic cancer – my wife took that final trip. The thought of any kind of sign was the furthest thing from my mind. But on the morning of her funeral, my sister and I spotted an eagle flying over our house.

It might not have been such a big deal if eagles were commonly seen in my area, but they aren't. It was the first – and last – time I had ever seen one in several years of living there. My next door neighbor, who is an avid bird watcher, also saw the eagle that morning and confirmed it was a rare sighting.

The eagle circled our home and perched itself in a large tree on our property. It stared down at us for the longest time – almost as if it wanted to make sure we saw it. "It's Wendy," my sister announced as we stared back at the eagle. Tears began to fill my eyes as we watched it finally fly away. "I think you're right. It's her sign to us: the eagle has landed."

HOMECOMING
By Anjali Pursai

Years ago, I left this house, ran from everything in it, my dad's last words repeating themselves on a loop in my mind, the funeral over so all I had to do was lock the door to my childhood home and flee, I thought, forever. Though he had left it to me, how could I walk the same halls he and Mom, gone just two years before, had walked since my birth? How could I sit at the same table where the three of us ate together? How could I? How could I?

Yesterday, the tenth anniversary of Dad's death dawned gray in my married home. I looked at my husband, whispered, "I can go back."

He hugged me and said, "Go." I drove the hundred miles from our small town to the countryside where I grew up, memories making their way back mile by mile.

Now in the still house, the creak of the closet door rings and lingers where once language and laughter filled the kitchen. Inside, I dig through musty shirts, jackets, and hats Dad wore over seasons as he chopped wood, trimmed plants, and shoveled snow to keep us connected with friends and neighbors. I search until I find it--the broom. Bringing it out, I gaze back at my path taken today from entryway to closet.

Such a long, slow journey to return here, I marvel at the familiar books calling my name and the handsome grandfather clock striking the hour. My steps had left footprints in the settling dust of ten years, so I began to sweep.

Broom bristles leave a series of lines and patterns. I sweep again and again to clean every inch. The swishing has a rhythm, and I find myself humming a tune. After what seems but a minute, the dust disappears; no longer do I see my footprints on the floor.

I return to the closet, open the door once more. The creak still startles, no longer lingers.

SONNET 84 WE DO SUCCEED
By E Baker

Evil works hard and, in ways tricky smart,
tries to pull us, all living, away
from Our Father, Our Creator, who made day,
night, and love; and with a loving, kind heart
taught us to know better than to dart
this way and that because of what some say
to lead us astray; instead, we do pray,
asking for guidance: Our Father which art
in Heaven, Hallowed be Thy Name . . . Lead
us not into temptation but deliver
us from evil . . . We pray these words and heed
them in our daily lives that we feed
with our constant Faith, belief, and prayer
And, Our Father willing, we do succeed

LISTEN UP
By Ann Gilbreth

Yes, it really happened at the checkout counter--many years ago. Something that changed my life.

He was a young man. I was next in line and he was waiting for the clerk to ring up his grocery items. While her hands busily picked up one and then another of his purchases, she gave him one of those quickie glances to acknowledge his presence, and asked the old trite "How are you today?" all without missing a single hand-to-item movement.

I'd heard it before, so I really didn't pay any attention until the young man replied quietly, but clearly, "I'm dying."

I cannot even try to describe my feelings. I could only stare at the man who was watching the clerk. She was watching his items and her register; but, without so much as another sightless glance at him, she nodded her head and replied, "That's good."

We both heard what she said. He then turned and looked into my eyes. I was totally stupefied by what I thought he had said, and now completely undone and speechless by the crass faux pas made by the clerk.

Spreading his hands wide and shrugging his shoulders, he gave me a crooked little half-smile and said, "You see! People don't really care."

While I stood there petrified, with my heart pounding in my ears, he simply picked up his sack of groceries and walked away.

By that time, I was suffering like I never had before because I didn't know if he had been proving a point, or whether he actually was---as he put it so bluntly---dying.

For me, it was the beginning of a new awareness of what people are saying, seriously or otherwise. I do not intend to go through something like that again. That young man could be dead now; or, he could be a rich old miser who remembers and laughs at his discovery that people don't care. I'll never know. I only regret that I could not find a voice back then to tell him he was wrong and that I cared even if I couldn't change anything for him. A kind word can't be rung up on the cash register, but it can ring throughout a lifetime inside a heart.

MEASURING UP
By Susan Mahan

My mother died when I was 14.

Life is a struggle, inch by blessed inch.
Mum's death was my yardstick.

Nothing closed the gaping divide--
not boys or proms or my childhood friends,
not the Beatles or Woodstock,
or the first man on the moon.

Nothing scaled the intensity--
not the Vietnam war or JFK;
not Robert Kennedy or Martin Luther King.
I concede that this is life.
I do not resort to hopelessness.

I gauge every instinct,
take calculated risks,
and weigh each decision
as if my life depends on it.

It does.

I married a fine measure of a man.
I raised my sons to be perceptive, funny, and kind.

Mum was on my mind every day,
but I never talked about her.
She even wrote poetry.
It's taken me this long to realize
that her spirit lives on

in me.

SURVIVE
By Jim Pahz

I'm going to die!

It was one of those eureka moments, the realization of one's own mortality. It wasn't something abstract, like *if a tree falls in the forest* kind of things. And it wasn't my usual gibberish like I've been uttering my whole life: *We're all dying. It's just a matter of **when** you die.* That was academic bullshit—Scholasticism. How many fairies can dance on the head of a pin sort of thing. Of course we're all dying, everyone knows that. But it's not real—it hasn't sunk in—not truly. They're just empty words. It's like the answer a 10-year-old might give you if you asked him what he plans to do in retirement. Whatever his answer, it doesn't matter—they're just words.

The doctor stood at the foot of my bed and looked directly at me. "This is serious," he said. "You can't leave the hospital yet. You've had a heart attack. You need to rest."

"I'm bored. I need to get home. I have things to do—important things."

"You're lucky to be alive. Your *things*, whatever those things are, can wait."

"When can I leave?"

The doctor turned to my wife. "Is something wrong with him? I mean besides the heart attack. Is he all right in his head?"

"He's driven, doctor. He's always been that way. It's like he's in a race with time. He can't get everything done in time."

"Well, if he doesn't slow down he's going to be out of time entirely. Maybe you can make him understand?"

"I'm going to try, doctor. I'll do my best."

"Good." He turned back to me, "I'll see you again this time tomorrow. Read a book or something. Watch television. Forget about leaving. You're the patient. I'll tell you when you can leave."

"Doctor," I asked. "If I hadn't gone to the emergency room... If I thought the chest pains would pass, like indigestion or gas, and stayed home, would I have been all right?"

"No, my friend, you probably would be dead. I can't say for certain, but that would be my guess."

"I see."

After the doctor left the room I asked my wife if she'd run home and get my volume of poems. I'm somewhat narcissistic and I like to read what I've created. When I had my book I opened it. I had written this particular poem about two years ago. At the time I thought it was cute. I thought I was clever because I was like Peter Pan, living in the moment. I would never grow up. "Listen to this," I said, as I began to read my poem to my wife:

MY DELICIOUS LIFE
I'm not productive today.
Not operating on all cylinders.

Caffeine deficiency.

Got a smoke?

I like a cigarette
in the morning
after breakfast
with coffee.

(I don't
lead by example)

Been thinking about a triple quarter – pounder
with cheese.
Maybe a Philly steak sandwich
drowning in Cheez Whiz.

Seems I got a problem
with volume.

But today
I don't have a sweet tooth.
Prefer
salt and fat.

*Think I'll spend the
morning at my favorite hangout --
the couch.*

*Reality TV
is what I like to watch.*

*Munching pork rinds,
ice cream, and
popcorn.*

*I'm not much
for exercise.
Controlling the zapper
is my idea
of a workout.*

*Why do I smoke?
Why not?
I'm a leader,
not a follower.
I believe in individual freedom.
Don't like people
telling me what to do.
Besides, everything good
is bad for you.
Somebody said that once,
maybe Confucius, Gandhi,
Captain Kangaroo,
the Muppets.*

*Anyway,
it's self-evident.*

*I heard once
a company could save
$ 340 per employee
each year
by keeping them physically fit.*

*But they won't save money
on me.*

> Not with my
> asthma,
> diabetes,
> and high blood pressure.
>
> So if you're going
> to ask me
> to wear a seat belt,
> don't bother.
>
> Besides
> those things aren't long enough to
> fit across my middle.
>
> I take two seats
> on an airplane.
>
> By the way,
> are you going to finish
> those fries?

God, could I use a smoke! I haven't smoked in many years, but I could use one now. There's something unsettling about facing the inevitable, the fact that you're not going to last forever. I put down my book of poetry and replaced it with the packet of information I received at the hospital. *Now*, it said, *be prepared to change your eating habits and your lifestyle, entirely.*

The irony didn't escape me. I was the irreverent poet. Was it a cosmic joke? The universe seemed to be out for revenge. It was telling me*: forget about sleeping in late this morning. When you get out of bed you're heading straight to your cardio-rehab session. Get ready for the treadmill and bicycle machine. Never mind that fancy restaurant you were looking forward to eating at tonight. Get used to the unpalatable taste of cardboard and sawdust. You may have believed you were* Peter Pan *and never growing up, but guess what?* WRONG. Your childhood days are over.

From the depths of despair, I had a thought. Maybe I wasn't being punished. This might be a Scrooge moment. Maybe it's similar to what happened to old Ebenezer. He could have groveled in self-pity and languished all night tossing in his bed sheets, but he didn't. He realized he might be one step closer to the grave, but he wasn't in it yet. And by that realization he was able to change his behavior and alter his future. Maybe I could too? Reclamation might be possible. My conclusion: I can get used to eating cardboard, if it means I can live to eat another meal. As it was revealed at the end of A Christmas Carol, *if ever a person knew the meaning of Christmas, it was old Ebenezer Scrooge.* And so it shall be with me! I appreciate life too much to just surrender. I want to survive. So I will adapt. I will say as Ebenezer did, "I'm not the man I was." I will change my behavior so I can stick around for a while longer. And then, when I'm 50 pounds lighter, and briskly walking five times a week, I will think about my progress. I will sit at the table and write a new poem. It might not be so clever.

HIS FAMILY'S CURSE
By Skip Hughes

As to its beginnings,
His history may not be uncommon.
For some decades he experienced paternal tyranny
Or a slowly degrading manifestation of it,
But failed to fight against it.
It was chiefly directed at sons of course,
For in those days daughters
Were primarily presumed to marry,
Keep house, give birth to and rear children.
Sons though, needed to face the real world,
And were expected to conquer, which however
Can be difficult under the curse of paternal tyranny.

Such oppression of sons ran in the family,
Again not uncommon, and in his case
May be traced three generations back,
Never to the benefit of any involved.
While progressively less severe
And less damaging to younger sons,
None entirely escaped its consequences.
Nor for that matter did the daughters
Completely lack this cruel experience.

Nonetheless this is not the history
Of an extended family,
So much as of an exploded family.
Against the long tradition
Of geographically close-knit clans
He and his four siblings,
An elder sister and three younger brothers,
Less than completely escaped the tyranny
In their teenage years, by running away from it.
Only the two youngest ever truly returned,
And then but temporarily.

Of the entire extended family from those
Paternal-paternal great-grandparents
Which led to his generation, all have now scattered
Hither and beyond, or passed on. Many ran away,
A few more than once, and some have since died.
Of a formerly large and prominent family,
None today remain in the old home town,
Or even in the same state or region.

Not one of those five siblings
Compiled a flawless record of marriage,
Each having experienced one divorce.
Three have not married again,
But he and one brother both
Have succeeded in second unions.
Neither did any of the five
Fail to falter professionally
At some juncture of their careers,
He several times in nearly as many professions.

For much of his life he has been a rolling stone,
Now in his eleventh state of residence,
Four times in one of them,
Twenty-five years in another,
And having visited all fifty states,
Plus four of the seven continents,
And resided in three of those.
He first married in his thirtieth year,
Into a family which also manifested
The stigmata of paternal tyranny.
The two of them were happy enough at first,
And produced one child, a daughter
Who was in her late teens when
Her parents divorced while in their fifties.

Some months after the divorce he encountered,
For a second time after four decades,
His high school sweetheart,
Who also was single at the time,
And quite romantically married her.
Whether this was fate or providence
None can more than conjecture,
But since losing her to a serious disease

After fourteen years of being together again,
He yet regards her presence twice in his life
As being among his most profound blessings.

The true miracle of this family,
The utter quietus of its protracted curse,
Transpired over several decades.
He and his three younger brothers
Are the sons of one surviving son of one son,
In those three generations, thus
The carriers of the curse, paternal tyranny.

To the five siblings including the elder sister,
Only daughters were born, seven of them altogether.
They have been referred to as "the revenge generation,"
After few daughters and many sons. In his generation
From his paternal grandparents came, in now inadmissible terms,
"A baseball team of boys and two cheerleaders."

As for the seven daughters of these five, all are fine women,
Each confident and accomplished in her own way.
While he no longer keeps track of the entire following generation,
Sons are coming along about equally with daughters.
He and his first wife contributed to the seven one daughter,
Now happily married, raising her own son and daughter,
Professionally busy and successful rather more
Than either of her parents, both as they were descended
From families that experienced the same curse.

As if these seven themselves were not enough blessings,
They also ended the family curse in a single generation.
Again was it providence, or fate?
Happenstance would seem unlikely,
But he delights in puzzling over it,
Though never reaching a satisfying conclusion.
Mainly he writes about it, and marvels at it all,
And he often thinks about his most profound blessings –
His daughter, and his twice-sweetheart second wife.

Thus this family's curse is no longer carried on,
And will die out with his generation.
So cantankerous is human nature however,
That one never knows when it may return,
But at least as a family ghost it is now banished.

While otherwise well equipped for success,
He has yet to achieve anything noteworthy,
But he is still trying. This is not altogether a bad thing,
Because remaining active is good at his age.
More than his daughter or the seven daughter-cousins,
Activity and a life-long penchant for humor, word-play,
May be his key to survival under adversity,
That which dogs every person and all humanity.

GRAVEN IMAGES
By John Manesis

"I no longer wanted to be an artist." Beto de la Rocha, L.A. Times

The painter slashed every canvas,
smashed the wooden frames
and torched his life's work
as though his soul was afire.
"But why?" his friends asked —
"Because I loved my art
more than God," he explained
and withdrew from the world.

For twenty years he searched
the Scriptures for an answer,
memorizing verse after verse.
When he lay upon the cot
and closed his weary eyes,
mad Nebuchadnezzar appeared,
babbling in the fields,
clouds of locusts swirled into Egypt,
Job's sores and blisters wept.

One night, deep in a chasm,
pressed against the dank walls,
over and over he yelled
for someone to raise him up
but the only sounds he heard
were the echoes of his own voice.
He understood what he had to do
and began the steep ascent,
inching upward, his swathed hands
clawing at the earth's mossy bones —
the dirt, stones, rocks, bare roots.

He awoke then,
drew back the shades
and waited at the window.
Morning finally came,
a garden of hues on the horizon
blazing with lilacs, roses, and blues
and as he watched the sun rise
relived the light in his landscapes.
The painter took up his brush again.

FLASHBACK
By Michelle Shen

A part of me only cares about moving forward, so I fall, I fall, I keep falling. As many Band-Aids cover my knees as rocks upon Yosemite trails. Stubborn, I scorn the stroller, ignore rugged rocks, small splinters, potential pain. I walk, I walk, I keep walking.

A part of me only cares about moving forward, a part of me I almost lost, a part of me I wish I never tamed; but the harder hardships made me crash and cry for help, rather than charging at them with my steely naïve mind and unwavering naïve spirit.

A part of me only cared about moving forward, so I never took time for marveling at waterfalls arched with rainbows, inhaling the smoke of burning juniper twigs, or eavesdropping on chattering birds as I do now. Both parts, one caring only about moving ahead and one relishing each memory, battled within me until I opened myself to balance.

SACRED SUNSHINE
By Rebekah Bernard

"You can only see sunshine after the rain, Rebekah," Lily whispered. I inhaled deeply and held my breath, pausing to mentally document this special moment of wisdom. Lily concluded our visit today with this nugget of truth as she finished recounting her life's many blessings. She was also gradually coming to terms with the ever growing cancerous tumor in her stomach that would soon end her life. Lily was a patient in our hospice inpatient facility and I was the spiritual counselor on the clinical care team assigned to help make her last days as dignified and comfortable as possible. This woman held a positive and grateful relationship with her cancer and inspired all staff that crossed her path. Lily's words at the end of our existential dialog struck a lasting cord within me as I reflected on my own beaming sunshine after a traumatic rainstorm.

My theoretical rain began on a snowy, cold morning. It was classified as a "state of emergency" snowstorm but, nevertheless, I was called into work. As I neared work, my car slid on black ice and crashed into a tree. I did not make it to work that day. The days that lay ahead required years of arduous physical and emotional personal trials, but I could not be more grateful for this divine intervention.

This traumatic car accident resulted in my being in a coma for nearly three weeks. I underwent brain surgery immediately following the accident, and was diagnosed with a permanent severe traumatic brain injury. The neurosurgeon notified my family that, if I woke from the coma, I may never operate beyond a three-year-old's brain level for the rest of my life. This brilliant man that saved my life advised my mother to look into nursing home options for me. My mother looked up at the neurosurgeon and spoke with absolute certainty: "You don't know my daughter." She saw and spoke with the eyes of her heart, and began seeing the sunshine that was possible while many saw only storm clouds and turbulence.

When I did wake from the coma, I immediately felt this overwhelming sense of spiritual clarity. Perhaps this coma was the most profound meditation I could ever experience. Soon, I would understand the meaning meditation would have in my life, marking mindfulness as the core of my healing journey.

As Jon Kabat-Zinn wisely surmised, "you can't stop the waves, but you can learn to surf." My healing did, in fact, begin at a three-year-old's brain level. I had to relearn everything, including how to use the right side of my body (which was paralyzed as part of my injury), how to read, how to put my hair in a ponytail, how to open a bottle of water with my right hand, how to navigate a keyboard solely with my left hand, etc. I did all this slowly, and with no expectations or judgment. I was experiencing a constant mindfulness practice, before I even really knew what mindfulness was. I truly could only stay in the present moment because this was all my brain would allow. I soon discovered I could not change or rush the healing process- and so, I had to learn how to ride the wave, and allow the sun to warm me each time I tried to catch the surf.

Eventually, mindfulness became the catalyst for my healing and growth. These unintentional practices allow me to trust and honor my brain injury. Trust that I would find anything that my brain injury seemed to be hiding. Trusting my memory and body to nurture the work I intended to do for others. I discovered the resilience in being still and just breathing. Something so simple and pivotal to life, yet so often overlooked. My grandest meditation- my coma- was me asking myself "what do you need, Rebekah?", and the Angels whispered "I need you- to share with others, to teach others, what's important."

Taking moment by moment, I nurtured my physical, emotional, and spiritual wellness. I was forced to live in a mindful way, because that's all my brain would permit, but even then knew my purpose was to help others the way I was helped. Each of the professionals that contributed to my holistic growth, mindfully took time to examine what would give me the greatest peace and possibility for my future. Combined with the loving support from family and friends, I became inspired and aimed to serve others early in my journey. First, I volunteered with a variety of helping non-profit organizations. With an honest understanding, I served those who came my way looking for support and guidance with coping through a healing journey and/or grieving the loss of certain abilities, relationships, or loved ones. My purpose on this Earth was clear, and I continued to follow the path which allows me to adapt to life's blessings, while providing guidance and healing to others in my care.

When the sunlight combines with the rain it can create a rainbow, this powerful force of hope. This rainbow is holistic in nature. The physical, mental, and emotional trauma that attempted to flood my life was met by moments of sunshine and possibility. As I discovered through my experience, education, work, and spiritual clarity – this possibility is always rooted in love.

In my hospice work as a spiritual counselor, I bear witness to the raw beauty in the psycho-spiritual transformation and the sun that shines at end-of-life. I observe patients examine the rain that has challenged their life and come to realize the sunshine exists in moments of pure, unconditional love. This is Sacred Sunshine. Lily was right- about her and about me. After the rain, sunshine

ABOUT THE CONTRIBUTORS

E Baker is an editor and writer who believes that one of poetry's gifts is how it triggers remembrances of our own — say, of survival. Her writings include "Two Left Shoes," *Living Lessons* (Whispering Angel Books); "Amazing Grace," Helium; "Chinua Achebe," *The New Crisis*; and "Smells Hurt" (monograph). She is author of two books: *So You Want a Higher Paying Job!* (New York City Board of Education, Grade 9 curriculum) and *101 Ways to Start a Business* (Earl Graves Publishing, NY). She is editor-writer for the Ray Hooper Design, NYC, Catalog 2014.

Judy Shepps Battle began writing poems long before she became a psychotherapist and sociology professor. Widely published in the USA and abroad during the sixties and seventies, she deferred publishing to concentrate on career and family. She continued to write both poetry and essays and is thoroughly enjoying sharing her muse once again.

Aashna Belenje, a first year student in Poetry Power, a private poetry institute in Campbell, CA, dedicated to professional training in the ancient art of poetry, has learned more about writing in five short months than all her years in school. Already, she has had one of her poems published in the renowned *Chautauqua Literary Journal* in New York. Also, she has had another of her poems win Third Place in the National League of American Pen Women's prestigious Soulmaking-Keats Literary Competition and will appear in a televised reading with other winners at the Koret Auditorium in San Francisco.

Rebekah Bernard is a grateful wife, whose experience and education has led her to work as a spiritual counselor with end-of-life care in hospice with an emphasis on psycho-spiritual, existential, and grief counseling. She has a Master's Degree in Counseling Psychology and has been a student of interdisciplinary spirituality for over a decade. Rebekah is featured as a contributing author in *365 Moments of Grace*. As she does this fulfilling work, Rebekah also teaches, speaks, counsels, and writes about living a love-centered, mindful existence. Please join her at rebekah-bernard.com and www.facebook.com/rebekahrbernard

Jane Blanchard lives and writes in Georgia. Her work has appeared in many journals, magazines, and anthologies in the United States and abroad as well as online. Her chapbook *Unloosed* is now available from White Violet Press.

Ann Reisfeld Boutte is a writer of poetry, essays, and feature stories. Her work has appeared in many publications including *Untamable City, The New Verse News, The Southern Poetry Anthology Volume IV, and Texas Poetry Calendars*. She has a Master's Degree in journalism and has worked as a feature writer for a daily newspaper and a national wire service. She was selected four times as a Juried Poet in the Houston Poetry Fest.

Lisa Braxton earned her MFA in creative writing from Southern New Hampshire University and Master of Science degree in journalism from Northwestern University. She is a former television and newspaper journalist and received an Emmy nomination during her career in broadcast journalism. She is the former president of the Boston chapter of the Women's National Book Association. Her short stories and essays have appeared in literary journals and anthologies including *Vermont Literary Review, Clockhouse, Chicken Soup for the Soul,* and *The Sun* magazine. She has completed her first novel, which is yet to be published. Her website address is www.lisabraxton.com.

Helen Carson lives with her husband in Southern California and has enjoyed careers in nursing and education. In her leisure time she pursues writing, reading, fine art photography, jewelry, design, needlework, mixed media art, travel, and time with family and friends. Ms. Carson's poetry has been featured in the literary journals *Tapestries, Third Wednesday Mosaic, Main Channel Voices,* the book *Living Lessons, and Voices of Breast Cancer*, an anthology, and *The Evening Street Review*.

Joy Case, M.Ed., is the Founder of Case Global Media Inc., a media company dedicated to building innovative, engaging platforms for companies to showcase their mission, vision and values, and to amplify their message through strategic video marketing. Prior to creating FunditTV.com, a web series for Crowdfunding, Joy has over thirteen years' experience as an educational leader in public schools (K-12) and over ten years' experience as a real estate agent. Joy's published book, a blueprint for a better world, is at www.AnIdeaNation.com.

Daawy, a law graduate from Nottingham Upon Trent University, began her writing career as a child earning top honors in a writing competition. In her debut novel, *From the Capital with Love*, she aspired to create a bridge between the Arabic and English worlds. Her book has been reviewed internationally and featured in several newspapers, magazines, radio stations, and television interviews. She is the proud mother of four children and has received several awards in figure skating and skiing. Her account name in Twitter, Instagram and LinkedIn is Daawy. She blogs at http://daawy.blogspot.com/

F. Anthony D'Alessandro was an associate editor of the defunct Italo-American Times. D'Alessandro's work has appeared in CUNY and the University of Texas publications. He's published in *Chicken Soup for the Father's Soul, Modern Bride, Teaching K-8, American School Board Journal, Newsday, San Francisco Chronicle, Christian Science Monitor,* and the *Tampa Tribune, Orlando Sentinel* to mention a few. In the spring of 2014, the Goose River Anthology published his book, *Brooklyn Birth: Sicilian Soul.* Currently, he's a correspondent for the Times of Sicily. He's taught at high school level for three decades and at the college level for 15 years. A retired high school Educator of the Year, he teaches at Valencia College and serves as Coordinator of Student Teachers for the University of Florida. Contact: Pamplona4@aol.com 1006 Sandlace CT, Celebration, FL 34747, 407-566-1727

Lola Di Giulio De Maci is a full-time writer now that her teaching days are behind her. Her stories appear in numerous publications, including multiple editions of *Chicken Soup for the Soul, the HCI Ultimate series, Reminisce magazine, the Los Angeles Times,* and *Holidays & Seasonal Celebrations,* a periodical for children. She enjoys crossword puzzles, books, journaling in a spiral notebook, handwritten notes/letters, her children, and new beginnings. Lola has a Master of Arts in education and English and continues writing from her loft overlooking the San Bernardino Mountains.

Karissa Dong has been published in literary journals nationwide, including *The Storyteller, Song of the San Joaquin,* and Eber and Wein Publishing's *Where the Mind Dwells: Contemplation*. Additionally, she has won several prizes for her work from the National League of American Pen Women and the Scholastic Arts and Writing Awards. She is passionate about fiction and journalism as well as poetic verse; her favorite novel since her younger years is J.D. Salinger's *The Catcher in the Rye*. She also loves travel; her favorite cities include Sorrento, Prague, Milan, and, of course, close to home, San Francisco.

Sharon S. Fulham's passion for writing became her lifelong companion following her at two universities where she earned a BA in Religion, and a MS in Education. As a Whispering Angel contributor in *Miracles & Extraordinary Blessings* by Lynn Johnston, two poems and two stories were published in 2014. Guidepost's *Mysterious Ways* magazine featured her Mysterious Moment in October/November, 2016 and her story Perfect Strangers in February/March, 2016. Elynne Chaplik-Aleskow, author of *My Gift of Now: A Collection of Short Memoirs* featured one of Sharon's quotes on the back cover of her book. Sharon's inspirational writing has appeared in *The Upper Room*, which is an interdenominational devotional guide. Her greatest joy is to uplift others and to celebrate life with her husband and son in North Carolina.

Constance Gilbert moved to Central Oregon to be a nearby Gramma and feel in love with the Cascade Mountains. She is a non-fiction writer with several published short stories. Music and books have been a major part of her life since age 7. She knits and plays canasta, Sudoku, and mahjongg to stimulate her little gray (brain) cells. However, studying scripture and Hebrew is her delight. At 72, Constance has many experiences and memories plus the beautiful mountains to inspire her writing. She is currently writing a book with the support of her Jerry Jenkins Writing Guild group. She can be reached at constancegilbert@gmail.com

Ann Gilbreth Before I ever went to school, I learned much from watching and listening to people, my pencil and tablet kept me busy pouring out my feelings in those early years of walking and talking with Jesus, my Lord. I went about publishing my own work. Books: *Be Still, Oh My Soul, Triangles, Let the Son Shine In, Tavish, Dream Man, Miracle In The Window,* and others. My articles, stories, and poetry have been published in numerous magazines, newspapers, religious publications, and *Christian Woman* (for over 50 years). My heart has to spill them out because they hurt me until I do.

Cona F. "Faye" Gregory-Adams is an award-winning writer of poetry, children's books, nonfiction, and short fiction. She has published internationally in newspapers, magazines, poetry journals and anthologies. She served as co-editor of the *On the Edge* MSPS annual anthology 2003-2012. Faye has published online in *Gateway to Jesus, Rogue Poetry Review, 37 Cents, Poetry Soup,* and others. She has print publications on *Canros, Ozarks Mountaineer, Mid-America Poetry Review, Art with Words, Wilderness (Korea), Cave Region Review, IDEALS, Mature Living, Birds and Blooms,* and others.

Lucinda Grey co-edited *Southern Poetry Review* for several years. She is the author of five books of poetry: *The Blue Hills: after the life of Maud Gonne*, winner of the Comstock Review Jessie Bryce Niles Award, *The Woman Who Has Eaten the Moon*, Wind Press, *Ribbon Around a Bomb*, which won the Quentin R. Howard Poetry Prize, Martin Flores and the House of Dreams, and *Letter to No Address*, Lamont Hall Prize, Andrew Mountain Press. She has won writer's residencies at the La Napoule Arts Foundation, La Napoule, France, The Valparaiso Foundation, Mojacar, Spain, and in Patzcuaro, Mexico.

Rene Hargett is a loving mother of three children and the favorite Gemmy of five grandchildren. She's been married to her husband for 14 years and currently resides in Indiana. Rene is a former victim of both child and spousal abuse. She writes not only as an outlet, but as a personal testimony to inspire others. She's living proof that with GOD'S help you can survive traumatic hardships and come out stronger than before. She is currently working on her autobiography, that will detail her journey from victim to victorious.

Juley Harvey is a former journalist (California and Colorado), and a prize-winning poet, with poems in more than 35 publications. Her most recent efforts include a third prize in Dancing Poetry's contest, an honorable mention in New Millennium Writings' 2015 *Shade of Infatuation*, Inclusion in Splattered Ink Press' *Celebrating Animal Rescue*, and Outrider Press' black-and-white series, *Embers and Flames*. Her poem, *A Life in Five Minutes*. featured within, received an honorary mention in the Estes Valley Library's first annual fire and flood memorial poetry contest, in 2014. She lives with her wire-haired terrier/Chihuahua, Moosie, in the gateway to Rocky Mountain National Park, near her 95-year-young father.

Anne Hill Ph.D. (a pseudonym) I am a therapist specializing in trauma recovery, victim advocacy, domestic violence, sexual assault and other women's issues. I've published numerous articles on these topics. In this volume I share my story in hopes of encouraging others who find themselves in similar situations. Due to my ex-husband, my true name needs to remain confidential. I can be reached, however, at annehill5yrs@gmail.com. My upcoming books, *God Spoke, I Listened: Volume 1: Surviving a Paranoid Psychopathic Husband* and *God Spoke, I Listened: Volume 2: Surviving a Paranoid Psychopathic Ex-husband, Corrupt Mental Health Officials and more* are in press.

Erika Hoffman pens mostly inspirational, non-fiction essays that appear in anthologies such as *Chicken Soup for the Soul* or in regional magazines like Sasee of Myrtle Beach. She's had her advice on writing humor appear in *The Writer* as well as having her essays on the craft get published in the online *Funds for Writers Magazine*. Although her niche seems to be the personal essay, she has crafted fictional stories which have been featured in *Deadly Ink Anthologies, Tough Lit. Magazines*, and *Page & Spine*. In total, Erika Hoffman has had 185 pieces published in the past six years. Before taking up her pen, she taught school for ten years and raised four children. Her degrees are from Duke University.

Skip Hughes' first poetry book, *Chuckleberry Chutney*, is scheduled for publication in autumn 2016 by WordTech Communications LLC. Skip's poetry has appeared in many anthologies and periodicals, and has been awarded prizes and also Summer Literary Seminars fellowships for writers' conferences in Kenya and Lithuania. He privately printed a chapbook, *A Pot of Message*, of which a few copies are still available (email: diffdrumr@gmail.com). Skip currently lives in Indiana, and previously resided on 10 other states. He holds an unusual academic distinction, having attended graduate school (on campus) at a major state university in every state beginning with "O."

Carolyn T. Johnson, a freelance writer from Houston, Texas, draws on her colorful life experiences for her short stories, poetry, and essays. She writes from the heart, the hurt, the heavenly, and sometimes the hilarious. Her work can be found in *The Houston Chronicle* and *The Austin American-Statesman* newspapers, as well as the *Whispering Angel Books Anthology* series, *Chicken Soup for the Soul, Yale Journal of Humanities in Medicine* and numerous other anthologies and e-zines. She can be reached at cetjohnson@comcast.net.

Roshanda Johnson came to know poetry at the age of six and developed an insatiable love for the written and spoken word. She has performed spoken word throughout the country, and her poetry has appeared in *Riversongs, American Society: What Poets See, Houston Poetry Fest's 2012 Anthology, Third Wednesday, Sierra Nevada, Tiger's Eye* and several other publications. She was recently nominated for The Pushcart Prize in Poetry. She is the author of the chapbooks *Unpredicted Prophecy* and *My Name* and would love for you to visit her at https://rizzo2d4.wordpress.com. Roshanda resides in Houston, Texas with her beloved dog, Bruce LeRoy.

Lynn C. Johnston is the author of *Angel's Dance: A Collection of Uplifting and Inspirational Poetry* and founder of Whispering Angel Books. She served as editor for *Hope Whispers, Living Lessons, Nurturing Paws, Littlest Blessings, Stir-Fried Memories,* and *Miracles & Extraordinary Blessings.* Her poems and essays have been published in several anthologies, including *Forever Friends, Timeless Mysteries, Antiquities, The World Awaits, Turning Corners,* and *Bridges.* Originally from New York, Lynn is a graduate of SUNY New Paltz. For more information, please visit www.whisperingangelbooks.com.

R. Todd La Flame lives in Ocoee, Fl. with his husband Glenn Lehman and their Boston Terrier/French Bulldog Bandit. He is head of the Warm Welcome Team at Windermere Union Church, UCC, and a Stephen Minister. He is part of the Emmaus Community and attends a meeting of The Greater Good Men's Breakfast Group. They are an Emmaus reunion group along with seeking ways to influence the wider community for good, by working in local prisons and schools. Todd has been legally blind since birth and HIV+ since at least 1990. He has spoken to college nursing students and care providers about how their treatment of people living with HIV/AIDS can help them to continue in care. He has also shared his story of finding spiritual light in a darkening world to church's and groups seeking to learn more about how they can reach out to the LGBT community. He may be reached via his Facebook page: Todd La Flame or via his E mail: toddglenn7@gmail.com

Mary Elizabeth Laufer was born in Buffalo, New York. She earned a degree in English from SUNY Albany, where she received the Leah Lovenheim Award for short fiction. Her stories, essays, and poems have been published in thirty-nine anthologies, the themes of her work ranging from a terrible teaching experience (*Perception: A New Adult Anthology*) to another hurricane nightmare (Best Short Stories from The Saturday Evening Post Great American Fiction Contest 2016). She lives in Central Florida, where writing helps her recover from years of being a navy wife, worrywart mother, hurricane survivor, and substitute teacher.

Theresa M. Leslie, a native Californian, has written verse for a many years and, for some time, has studied with an award-winning poet at Poetry Power, a California institute dedicated to professionalism in this ancient art. Literary journals nationwide have published her poems, including *New York's Soul Fountain* and *Illinois' West Ward Quarterly.* She has also won Second Prize in the prestigious Voices of Lincoln National

Poetry Contest. When not writing, Theresa spends time with her family and plays ice hockey.

Susan Mahan has been writing poetry since her husband died in 1997. She is a frequent reader at poetry venues, including the Boston Public Library and the Catbird Café in Weymouth. She has self-published four chapbooks, including, *Missing Mum*, 2005, and *World View*, 2009. She has been published in a number of anthologies, including *Kiss Me Goodnight, Solace in So Many Words, Living Lessons, Crave It: Writers and Artists Do Food, Cradle Songs: An Anthology About Motherhood*, and *The Widows' Handbook*.

John Manesis is a retired physician, whose poetry has appeared in over 90 literary publications, including *Wisconsin Review, North Dakota Quarterly, California State Poetry Quarterly* and *Footwork: Paterson Literary Review*. He has had five poetry books published. The poem, *Graven Images"* was included in his first book, *With All My Breath*.

Aarya Mecwan is passionate about computer science, music, literature, learning, and the world in general. She remains grateful for her artistic inclinations, especially in poetry. She is confident poetry gives her a depth and understanding of the world that will be of help in any path she takes in life. A second year student in Poetry Power, she has placed twice in the National League of American Pen Women's annual Soul-making Contest and earned Third Place in Voices of Lincoln annual poetry contest. She has also had her work published in Illinois, New York, Utah, and California.

Rosemary McKinley has always been intrigued by anything historical. When she moved to the North Fork of Long Island, New York, she felt compelled to write about Colonial America and later. Her first book, *101 Glimpses of the North Fork and Islands*, highlights the area in vintage pictures and captions. Her second book is a children's historical novella, *The Wampum Exchange*, depicting life in 1650, Southold through the eyes of an English boy and a Corchaug Indian. Their chance meeting and aftermath changes their lives forever. Both books are available on amazon.com and B&N.com. Her writing story has appeared in *Women of Distinction Magazine* and the *Suffolk Times 50+ Magazine* in 2015. Her short stories, essays and poems have been published online by the Visiting Nurse Association of Long Island and in *Lucidity, LI Sounds, Clarity, canvasli.com, Peconic Bay Shopper, Fate Magazine, Examination Anthology, Wormwood Press, Good Old Days Magazine, Newsday,* and *The Poet's Arts*. Two short stories are available on Smashwords.com

Bridget McNamara-Fenesy lives in the Pacific Northwest, where she works as an independent business consultant when she is not pursuing her passion of writing. Bridget received her BA from the University of Notre Dame, and her JD from the University of Denver. She has been published in *The Sun literary magazine, Fate Magazine, Chicken Soup for the Soul*, as well as other local and national publications. She is thankful to her family for providing such a rich source of material for her muse. Bridget can be reached at bridgetmcnamara@comcast.net.

Beckie A. Miller began writing when desperate to find a way of venting the devastating emotional pain from the death of her 18-year-old son, Brian, who was robbed and killed in October of 1991. The more she wrote the more she needed to write. She is chapter leader of Parents of Murdered Children, in Phoenix, Arizona, for the past 23 years and has won numerous awards for her work with crime victims. This is the fourth series of Whispering Angel Books she has had stories published in *Nurturing Paws* and *Living Lessons*. She has also been published in other books, i.e. *Every Woman Has A Story, Dear Mom, I Always Wanted You To Know, Unsent Letters*, several magazines and guest articles in the *Arizona Republic*, as well as poetry.

Sheree K. Nielsen is Author/Photographer of the 2015 Da Vinci Eye Award Winner, *Folly Beach Dances*, a 'healing' coffee table book about South Carolina inspired by the rhythm of the sea and her journey with lymphoma. Over the years, she's received many awards for her writing, photography, and poetry. Publications include *AAA Southern Traveler, AAA Midwest Traveler, Carolina Go! Missouri Life*, and anthologies, newspapers, and websites across the nation and Caribbean. When not writing, she's often seen riding around town with her two goofy dogs, sipping non-fat cappuccinos. She blogs 'all things' inspirational at www.shereenielsen.wordpress.com, tweets @ShereeKNielsen and @follybeachdance. The book's website is www.beachdances.com

Jim Pahz is a poet and writer of prose. He has written several books, some by himself and some with his wife, Cheryl Pahz. They live in Central Michigan in the middle of the mitten. Jim didn't start writing short stories and novels until after retiring from a 33-year teaching career at Central Michigan University. The couple's website is jcpahz.com. All of his books can be found on Amazon.com. His most recent book is a collection of short stories entitled *Tale of a Simple Man*.

Anjali Pursai was accepted into the prestigious workshop devoted to poetry, Poetry Power in the San Francisco Bay Area, taught by an award winning poet. Since that time two years ago, she has earned several publications, such as *Chautauqua Literary Magazine* in New York, and awards, such as the National League of American Pen Women. She has also been invited to read her work aloud at a number of well-known Bay Area locations, such as the Koret Auditorium at the Main Branch of the San Francisco Library. She grows more and more enthusiastic about the art of poetry, both writing and presenting it.

Diana Raab is an award-winning author of eight books and over 600 articles and poems. She's a memoirist, poet, blogger, essayist, and educator. She facilitates workshops on writing for healing and transformation, the focus of her doctorate research in psychology. She's been writing since the age of 10 when her mother gave her her first journal to cope with her grandmother's suicide. *Lust* is her most recent poetry collection. Her non-fiction book, *Writing for Lust* is forthcoming in 2017. Raab is a regular blogger for *Psychology Today*, *The Huffington Post*, and *PsychAlive*. Her website is dianaraab.com.

Carol J. Rhodes is president of C.R. Business Services, a freelance literary/technical editor, business consultant, and instructor of business writing courses. Her short stories, personal essays, poetry, non-fiction articles, plays, and book reviews have been widely published. Included in her credits are: *The Houston Chronicle. Christian Science Monitor, Chicken Soup for the Girlfriend's Soul and Texas Poetry Calendar.*

Kathleen A. Ryan is a retired 21-year veteran of the Suffolk County Police Department in New York. A breast cancer survivor, Kathleen lives on Long Island with her husband and two children. She volunteers with Crime Stoppers of Suffolk County, Inc. and A Wing and A Prayer Animal Rescue. A Macavity and Derringer Award finalist, Kathleen is the President of Long Island Sisters in Crime (LI SinC); a member of NY/TriState SinC. Mystery Writers of America, and Public Safety Writers Association. Visit her on Facebook, her website: http://www.kathleenaryan.com, Instagram and Twitter @katcop13.

Michelle Shen, a senior in high school, has written poetry since fourth grade and is enrolled in her fourth year of the program Poetry Power. She has won prizes for her poetry in contests sponsored by California Federation of Chaparral Poets, Scholastic Art and Writing Awards, and the Soul-Making Keats Literary Competition. She has also earned publications in literary journals such as *Song of the San Joaquin* in California, *The Storyteller* in Arkansas, *Westward Quarterly* in Illinois, and *Chautauqua Literary Journal* in New York. She gathers inspiration from her loving family, travel experiences, war stories, Greek mythology, and nature's beauty.

Beth SKMorris is the author of two poetry books, *In Florida* (2010) and *Nowhere to be Found* (2015). Her poems have appeared in *Artemis Journal, Avocet, Lingerpost, Poetica, the PEN,* and anthologies by White Oak Press and the International Library of Poetry. *Spring Street* is part of a new book of poetry she is currently completing called, *Above the Pile*, which speaks to her experience as a volunteer at the Supply Center Warehouse which served the first responders and recovery workers at Ground Zero post 9/11. Beth is a member of the Hudson Valley Writers Center, Sleepy Hollow, NY.

Deborah Lamkin Smith has a passion for those who have suffered the loss of a loved one. Her daughter Jennifer, and only child, died in 1998 as the result of a car accident. As a healthcare professional she has had the opportunity to console many of those suffering grief. She loves to go camping, fishing, and bike riding. The beauty of the landscape there inspires her acrylic paintings.

Ruth E. Smith lives in Orlando, FL and is the mother of three daughters, Laura Jo Anna, and Diana. A lifelong learner, she is inspired by reading the Bible, affirmations, and stories of survivors. She enjoys creative writing, drawing, oil painting, collecting quotes and photography. She is a member of NAMI (National Alliance of Mental Illness) and her passion is encouraging others to overcome despite what obstacles they may face in life.

Judith Lyn Sutton, a previous contributor to *Whispering Angel Books*, has devoted her life to the written word. With an M.A. in English and selection as a private student by poet luminary Diane Di Prima, Judith has won poetry awards and publication nationwide. She ranks appearing in an anthology of 20 poets, including Jack Kerouac, as her highest honor. After a 40-year teaching career, she founded Poetry Power, a private institute in CA to strengthen poetic voices. Also a playwright and producer, she spent 20 years leading a regional theater warmly received by Bay Area audiences and critics alike.

Rebecca Taksel is the author of *Come Away*, a novel on the 2016 list of Little Feather Books. She was contributing editor of the *Redwood Coast Review*, where her essays and memoir pieces appeared from 2004 to 2014. Rebecca was included in the Whispering Angel anthology, *Nurturing Paws*. She contributed to Animals Agenda and Natural Home magazines. She has recently begun to write poetry and has had a poem accepted for an anthology on recovery from addiction to be published by

Tuliptree Press for Recovery Wyoming. Rebecca invites readers of Soul Survivors to visit her on Facebook.

Carolyne Van Der Meer is a journalist, public relations professional and university lecturer. She has undergraduate and graduate degrees in English Literature from University of Ottawa and Concordia University respectively, and has a Graduate Certificate in Creative Writing from the Humber School for Writers. She has published journalistic articles, essays, short stories and poems in publications in Canada, India, Ireland, Italy, the U.K. and the U.S. New work is forthcoming in Germany. Her first book, *Motherlode: A Mosaic of Dutch Wartime Experience*, was published by Wilfrid Laurier University Press in 2014. Her second book, a collection of poetry entitled *Journeywoman*, will be published in 2017 by Toronto-based Inanna Publications. She is currently at work on a young adult fiction novel.

Jean Varda's poetry has appeared in: *The California Quarterly, The Berkeley Poetry Review, Lucid Stone, Poetry Motel, The Santa Fe Sun, Avocet A Journal of Nature Poetry, River Poets Journal* and *Prompt* online literary magazine. She has published 5 chapbooks of poetry, most recently, *She Was Attached To Symmetry*, by Sacred Feather Press. Her poem *Sister Morphine* that appeared in *Red River Review* was nominated for a Pushcart Prize. She lives in Greenfield, MA, where she works as a poet and collage artist.

Wendy Wolf When I was young, books saved me. They provided sanctuary and escape, which made me believe that being an author was one of the noblest things anyone could do. So, I plop my heart on the page and put it out into the world, filling my stories with messages like this: Live with integrity and kindness. If you love animals, don't eat or wear them; there's already too much killing and cruelty in the world. Read. Go outside. Create something. Be gentle with yourself and others. Life can be hard—may your happiness (far) outweigh your sorrow.

Cherise Wyneken's prose and poetry have appeared in a variety of publications, two full collections of poetry, two poetry chapbooks, a spiritual memoir, a novel, a children's book, a children's audiocassette, and *Stir-Fried Memories*, stories from my life, winner of Whispering Angel Books 2012 nonfiction contest. Archives from her poetry column for the Oakland Examiner's online issue can be found at: www.examiner.com/poetry-in-oakland/cherise-wyneken and her poem, *Re-borne*, was nominated for the 2012 Poetry Pushcart Prize.

Alina Zeng has fallen in love with the arts: photography, painting, music, dance, and poetry. She has written poems for four years because she enjoys expressing important ideas about life in a creative way; she became serious about it when admitted as just an eighth grader into the Poetry Power workshop in Campbell, which had never before enrolled anyone in middle school. Since then, she has achieved publication nationwide and earned a number of awards.

WE WANT TO HEAR FROM YOU

Has one or more of the stories touched your heart? Has it made you think differently about your own situation? We would like to hear your thoughts or comments.

Do you have a short story or poem that you'd like to see in a future Whispering Angel Book? If so, please go to our website for upcoming book topics and submission guidelines.

Whispering Angel Books is dedicated to publishing uplifting and inspirational stories and poetry for its readers while donating a portion of its book sales to charities promoting physical, emotional, and spiritual healing. If you'd like more information, please contact us.

Follow us on Twitter: @whisperangelbks and like our Facebook page: Whispering Angel Books

To contact us or to order additional books, please visit:

www.whisperingangelbooks.com

www.ingramcontent.com/pod-product-compliance
Lightning Source LLC
Chambersburg PA
CBHW020652300426
44112CB00007B/342